young true woman

BETSY GÓMEZ
EDITOR

young true woman

STAND FIRM IN A WORLD THAT TRIES TO SEDUCE YOU

FOREWORD BY LAURA GONZÁLEZ DE CHÁVEZ

KREGEL PUBLICATIONS

Young True Woman: Stand Firm in a World That Tries to Seduce You

Published by agreement with the literary agency Wolgemuth & Associates, Inc.

Italics in Scripture quotations indicate the author's added emphasis.

Cataloging-in-Publication Data is available from the Library of Congress.

ISBN 978-0-8254-4930-7, print
ISBN 978-0-8254-4932-1, epub
ISBN 978-0-8254-4931-4, Kindle

Printed in the United States of America
25 26 27 28 29 30 31 32 33 34 / 5 4 3 2 1

CONTENTS

Contributors

Betsy Gómez is a writer and speaker on a mission to help women connect the gospel to everyday life. She wrote *Soy Niña* (*I'm a Girl*) because she believes biblical womanhood is all about knowing God and living for His glory. She served at Aviva Nuestros Corazones (Revive Our Hearts), leading Joven Verdadera (Young True Woman) and equipping young women to stand firm in God's truth. These days, Betsy cohosts *El Podcast de los Gómez* with her husband, Moisés (who's also a pastor at Ekklesia in Dallas). Together, they dive into why following Jesus is worth it. Their home is filled with love, laughter, and just the right amount of chaos, thanks to their four kids—Josué, Samuel, David, and Grace. More than anything, Betsy wants every girl to know this: Christ is the treasure your heart has been searching for—seek Him, know Him, and live for Him! Curious to learn more? Check out losgomez.org.
Instagram: @betsytgomez

Aylín Michelén de Merck is known and loved by God through Christ. Nothing else matters more than the way He sings over her, giving her rest, joy, and deep safety in His love. She is married to Ethan and a mama to three brave and adventurous kids. Through the Spirit, Aylín is devoted to knowing, loving, and embodying Jesus. Following His lead has meant creating flourishing spaces for her family's unique needs, living cross-culturally for over twenty years, and providing whole-person soul care for gospel workers and their families—both in the States and abroad.
Instagram: @aylinmerck
Substack: https://open.substack.com/pub/aylinmerck

Erin Davis is a writer and teacher passionately committed to getting women of all ages to the deep well of God's Word. She is the author of more than twenty books and Bible studies, including *7 Feasts, Fasting & Feasting*, and *A Parent's Guide to Lies Boys Believe*. Hear her teach on the *Deep Well with Erin*

Davis podcast. When she's not writing, you can find Erin chasing chickens and children on her small farm in the Midwest.
Instagram: @thedeepwellwitherindavis

Kelly Needham is the author of *Friend-ish* and *Purposefooled* and cohost of the *Clearly* podcast alongside her husband, Jimmy. She and Jimmy live in the Dallas area with their five children. You can learn more about Kelly at jimmyand kelly.com or on her social media.
Instagram: @kellyneedham

Susi Bixby has been married to Matthew since 1998, and together they have three adult children. Desiring to live God's plan for her life, she dedicates the greatest part of her energy to her family and local church body alongside Matthew, who is a pastor at Iglesia Bautista la Gracia (Grace Baptist Church) near Monterrey, Mexico. She loves to study and share the Word of God. You can listen to her parenting podcast in Spanish, *Crianza Reverente*, at crianzarever ente.com.
Instagram: @susibixby

Kristen Clark and Bethany Beal are sisters, lifelong friends, founders of Girl Defined Ministries, and authors of *Girl Defined*, *Love Defined*, and *Sex, Purity, and the Longings of a Girl's Heart*. These tall girls from Texas are passionate about biblical femininity and love to impart God's truth through one-on-one discipleship. They also love to write, teach, blog, and post videos on YouTube. They are avid and competitive sportswomen, especially when it comes to basketball, and are always ready for outdoor adventures. When they are not writing or speaking, you can find them spending time with their extensive family or relaxing at a local café.
Instagram: @girldefined

Laura González de Chávez is the wife of Fausto and lives in Illinois. Her passion is to disciple women of all ages with the solid foundation of God's Word and to encourage them to live according to the faith they have embraced. She currently leads the ministry of Aviva Nuestros Corazones (Revive Our Hearts), a role that has helped her reach women of her generation with the message of the gospel and biblical womanhood. Alongside her husband, she hosted the weekly radio program *Un Hogar Sobre la Roca* for many years, seeking to contribute to redeeming God's design for the family. She has a daughter, Sarah, who is married to Jonathan, and five beautiful grandchildren: Zoë, Noah, Joy, Levi, and Vera Grace.
Instagram: @lauragonzdech

Nancy DeMoss Wolgemuth has experienced the life-changing power of the truth and wants to see others experience it too. She is the founder and lead Bible teacher for Revive Our Hearts, a ministry dedicated to calling women of every age to freedom, fullness, and fruitfulness in Christ. Nancy and her husband, Robert, live in Michigan. They are grateful for the joy of sharing their lives together and of serving the Lord and others.
Instagram: @nancydemoss

FOREWORD

When I met Betsy, I knew that, somehow, God would link our lives in ministry. And so it was. Years later, the Lord led her to serve as part of the Revive Our Hearts team. Her joy, empathy, ideas, and creativity entered our lives like a ray of sunlight through the window.

What great joy it brings me to see God's beautiful work in Betsy's life! He transformed her into a God-fearing woman, passionate about the gospel, and a godly wife, mother, and servant. I'm so happy to see how the fruits of embracing the gospel and the call to biblical womanhood unfolded so naturally and invitingly in her life. I love witnessing how she has submitted her life to His purposes and how she has harnessed the gifts and talents God has granted her to minister to the young women of her generation.

Her passions are sharing the beauty of the gospel and helping young women find their identities in Christ. Her message is necessary not only for girls but also for all of us who have placed our faith in Him.

We are in the end times, and this book contains a critical message. The sin of our hearts, added to the ideologies and philosophies that govern this world and shape our thinking, has caused confusion, misdirection, and even disaster in the lives of many young women. It has never been as important as it is now to know the truth.

Perhaps you are asking yourself the same question that Pilate once asked Jesus: "What is truth?" (John 18:38). The truth is a person—Jesus. He is "the way, the truth, and the life" (14:6), and "He may be found" (Isaiah 55:6 NIV). His will for you is contained in the Bible—the book that will guide you to wise and safe paths, paths that will lead you to the freedom, fullness, and abundance you so long for.

I invite you to open your heart and accept the challenge presented to you by the authors of *Young True Woman*. It is my prayer that the Spirit of God will open your eyes to His truth and that this will captivate you, inclining your heart to obey it. I pray that He will show you how this truth can transform your understanding, helping you to encounter His good, kind, and perfect will for every part of your life (Romans 12:2).

May God bless you abundantly in the reading of this book and help you to mold your life around His truth!

Laura González de Chávez
Director of Aviva Nuestros Corazones

Don't Skip the Introduction

Betsy Gómez

No one can travel to the past, but when I think of my "wonder years," I imagine what could happen if I went back twenty-five years and met up with my younger self. How much advice I would give her! I don't have many photos of those years, but one thing I do remember is the passion with which I lived. I had a strong desire to please God, but my mind had not been transformed by His Word. My ears were open to all kinds of voices—at home, at church, in school and college, and everywhere else.

I am a millennial, but young people did not have smartphones even at that time. The only thing I carried was a pager. (I know you have no idea what that is, but you can look it up on the internet.) Believe it or not, at that time there were no social media platforms. They started up when I was in my early twenties, but they weren't widely used until years later. My contact with the outside world was limited to TV, radio, and magazines. But that was enough to expose me to a great number of lies that shaped the way I lived.

My younger self—with a single mother who did everything possible to raise me and with a believing aunt who took me to church and shaped my love for Christ—tried to figure out life and conquer the pressures that I felt. Sometimes I was focused on what was important, and other times I was all over the place because I really wanted to be accepted by others.

If I were to meet my younger self, no doubt she would be singing. Or she would be humming a popular hymn from church that essentially told God that all her life, all she dreamed of and all she hoped to be, was in him. Or maybe she would be imitating Thalia's song, telling the world that she didn't care about what she did or said—that was how she was and she'd never change. Ha, ha! What a contradiction! At that time, I was very close to the truth, but the world was very seductive, and it drew me in. I sincerely thought it would never do me any harm to be exposed to all its ideas.

Without a doubt, that was a serious mistake. Over time, that girl gave in to messages enticing her to live for herself and to trivialize the holiness of God and the importance of living in purity. Little by little, she devalued the traditional roles of marriage. She began to see motherhood as an obstacle in the way of success and to mold her faith around a message of which she was the center.

I would like to tell my younger self so many things that a single meeting would not be enough. I would need to bring her everything in writing. Well, I would first have to convince her of the urgency of my message, because at that time, I did not like to read. Do you know what I would write to her? I would write to her about things that might seem unimportant at that point in life but that are crucial for her well-being. I'd tell her where every decision I made—driven by the world and my flesh—had led me. I'd show her the only path to true freedom.

I would warn her of the danger of handing over her heart—which is deceptive and, by nature, obscures the truth—to a world that wishes to ensnare it in lies that lead to destruction. I would want to tell her so many things!

I Don't Need to Travel to the Past

But the truth is that I could only do so in my imagination. Life is not a fictional movie. It is impossible to travel back in time to change things, and in truth, there is no need to do so. God, in His goodness and sovereignty, allowed me to live all of those experiences, and He has used them for my benefit and His glory. What I can do is provide you with this work, which contains the truths that I would have liked to know a long time ago.

So, imagine that my friends and I are bringing you these truths from the future to warn you. My prayer is that you might read them as if they were a life-and-death message because that is what they are. I beg you to approach each chapter with your heart set on learning, because what we want to share with you comes not only from hearts that wish to see you walk in the truth but also from the Word of God. Let me assure you that you will get more from this book if you read it with a Bible in hand.

We hope that when you meet the truth, you will be able to recognize it and submit your life to it. May what happened to Pilate—not recognizing the truth even though He was right in front of him—not happen to you. What do you know about this encounter?

We will look at it together in the first chapter to discover what it has in common with our generation.

PART 1

An Encounter with the Truth

One

What Is Truth?

BETSY GÓMEZ

A Blind Encounter with the Truth

Go get your Bible—physical or digital—and read John 18:33–38. This is a surprising encounter. For a long time, I didn't understand what really happened here. Pilate received Jesus from the hands of the priests to judge Him and later submitted Him to them to be crucified. But first, they had a conversation that seemed more like a game of questions, and if we examine the scene carefully, we will see the contrasts that took place there. An earthly governor who "decides" the fate of the supreme authority of all existence. An unjust man who "judges" the author of all justice. A blind man with a clouded understanding in the face of the Light of the World.

In his attempt to figure out who this man was, Pilate asked Him whether He was king, but Jesus's answer puts an end to his curiosity.

> Pilate said, "So you are a king?"
>
> Jesus responded, "You say I am a king. Actually, I was born and *came into the world to testify to the truth*. All who love the truth recognize that what I say is true."
>
> "What is truth?" Pilate asked. (verses 37–38)

Pilate reacted with a final question: "What is truth?" We know he didn't wait for Jesus to answer because he had not finished asking and already his feet were directed toward the exit door. Either because he was convinced there was no answer, or, more likely, because he did not want to hear it.[1]

This scenario has been repeated throughout the history of humanity. Pilate's insolence and cynicism have echoed in the minds of the philosophers who have shaped the thinking of our generations.

Through the years, humans have asked themselves what truth is, but only in order to define it according to their own reasoning and imagination. And do you know what the only thing they have found is? Confusion and deceit. Instead of looking straight to the source of absolute truth, they have tried to look aside in order to avoid it and numb their understanding. Just like Pilate, humans do not want to learn the truth. They prefer to filter it to avoid the harshness of things as they really are.

If you go into your social media or turn on the TV or radio, you will see Pilate's insolence interwoven in the way this world thinks. The sad part is that these currents of thought are not only filtered through the media but also hidden in our hearts. They are like sugarcoated poisonous candies. They are such attractive thoughts, so logical and accessible, that they make us forget the power they have to destroy us. I'm talking about thoughts like these:

- I define my own truth!
- Don't try to define me by your personal truth!
- No one can judge me.
- The truth is what works for me or makes me feel good.
- The truth is what I have been taught.
- You offend me if you do not accept and respect my truth.
- The truth is relative. Everyone can decide the truth that is "right" for them.
- The truth is subjective. Everyone has the right to define it according to their experience or reasoning.

These ideas are so familiar to us that it's difficult for us to discern whether they are correct or not. Just like a video clip I saw recently in which a young female artist was singing at the top of her lungs, telling people not to mess with her freedom against a backdrop showing "sexually empowered" women. It will always be easier to appeal to a personal truth to excuse immoral behavior, which goes against God's plan. What she cannot see is that what they call freedom actually binds them in chains.

I challenge you to join me in unmasking culture's lies. We will explore how Pilate's attitude in the face of truth has infiltrated our hearts. But first I should warn you that we will expose ourselves to the fact that the truth is not going to make us feel like we're on a gentle sleigh ride down a mountain and into green meadows filled with colorful flowers. There will probably be moments when it feels like climbing a rocky peak against a fierce wind.

Maybe the same thing that happened to me will happen to you. I felt like everything that had defined me for years was being taken away. I had to let go of things that I had treasured. Sometimes, this was delightful, but other times, because of my pride, it has been painful. But I admit that I have examined what I've left behind and realized that it was all unnecessary baggage that was weighing down my life and robbing me of freedom and joy.

Like Eyeless Zombies

This is nothing new. Ever since humans were created, the truth has been under attack, and our sin has made us prone to reject and disobey it. Below we'll spend some time looking at the darkest moment in the history of God's people. Take my hand and come with me—you'll see how everything makes sense later.

In the first three chapters of Genesis, we see a very clear picture: God, the author of creation, took the initiative to reveal Himself to man and woman. His instructions were true and precise. Then the deceiver entered the scene and found a place in the hearts of God's creations. Until that moment, humankind had everything they needed and knew only the truth. But that didn't last long. Stop for a moment and read Genesis 3:1–14.

Everything changed forever when their hearts echoed questions of the goodness of God ("Did God really say . . . ?"), when they gave their ears over to hearing a whispered lie ("You won't die!"), and when their curious minds gave in to the invitation to usurp the throne of the Creator ("You will be like God").

They accepted the poison that came out of the mouth of the Father of Lies and disobeyed God—the single source of all that is true. They went from living in a paradise filled with splendor to living in a profound abyss of darkness. Their eyes dimmed until they ceased to see the truth that was so clearly before them. On that horrible day, sin extinguished all light within humanity, and from that moment, we began our journey into darkness—a darkness that our fallen hearts have come to love.

But God, in His love, did not leave us there. He promised that He would send His Light to restore everything; He promised that One would come who would conquer the power of death (verse 15). He chose a people from which the Savior would come, and despite the darkness that surrounded them, He guided them with His truth. Their journey shows that, although they put their trust in God's promise, their hearts insisted on rejecting the truth and loving the darkness.

- Abram and Isaac tried to save their lives by lying and hiding the truth (Genesis 12:10–20; 26:6–11).
- Because of their jealousy, the sons of Jacob sold Joseph and concealed the truth (Genesis 37).
- When God communicated His truth to Moses, the people gave themselves over to darkness and worshipped an idol, putting aside the truth they had received from God. By their actions, they showed the darkness that reigned in their hearts (Exodus 32:8).
- David hid his sin until the prophet Nathan confronted him with the truth (2 Samuel 12:1–23).
- Solomon was granted great wisdom, but he decided to put aside the truth and gave himself over to lies that entangled his heart in sin (1 Kings 11:1–13).
- Jonah fled because he refused to tell the truth to a nation that was in darkness (Jonah 1:1–3).
- God sent prophets with the truth of His Word, but the people rejected them (Nehemiah 9:26).

The list could continue because this has been the pattern of humanity right up to the present. We insist on distancing ourselves from the truth. We love darkness more than light. We suppress the truth out of love for our sins.

God promised that He would send His Light to restore everything.

But God is different. He did not hide the sin of His people. He did not use Instagram filters to make them look better. He constantly revealed how dark the condition of humankind was and how great was humanity's need for a savior. Again and again, God revealed His truth and the people rejected it (Romans 1:18–19) just like when someone wakes you up in the middle of the night and you hide your face because your eyes cannot bear the light.

And this is not just the history of biblical characters that you might've learned in Sunday school. It is your history. It is our history. From the moment sin brought death to humankind, we became eyeless zombies who seek dark places to live in. If we are separated from the truth, we look quite alive on the outside, but our spiritual reality is horrible. We pull ourselves together and try to look good, but the stench of the lies that dominate us is going to come through one way or another.

It's incredible that God has not looked away from us or ignored our needs. He fulfilled His promise and, in due time, sent the light that eliminates all darkness.

> I am the light of the world. If you follow me, you won't have to walk in darkness, because you will have the light that leads to life. (John 8:12)

> The Word gave life to everything that was created,
> and his life brought light to everyone.
> The light shines in the darkness,
> and the darkness can never extinguish it.
> (1:4–5)

"The light shines in the darkness, and the darkness can never extinguish it." The people for whom the Savior came did the same as had been done for generations: fled from it instead of running toward the Light. Worse still, they conspired to destroy it, like eyeless zombies who reject the only hope in life (3:19–21).

This was Pilate's situation when he received Jesus from the hands of blind people. The saddest part is that he was just as blind as they were. And, of course, it is so easy to see this like a Netflix movie and say, "What a dumb man! How could he fail to see?"

But how can you be sure there is not a Pilate in you? How do you know you are not so used to the lies of this world that you don't recognize the truth when it is in front of you? Are you turning your back on the Light because your eyes are full of darkness?

Unmasking the Lies

That was how things were with me. Like I said in the introduction, although I was a church girl and truly wished to devote my life to God and His work, my heart was saturated with lies about God, the work of Christ, and my identity and design as a woman. I couldn't tell the difference between the truth and the lies. My faith in Jesus was so mixed in with worldly thinking that I didn't know how to distinguish biblical truth from false, humanistic reasoning.

Don't worry. I'm not about to give you a philosophy lesson, but I do want you to be able to see that each decision, no matter how simple, has its origin in your definition of the truth. How you approach the truth affects all areas of your life. Whether you realize it or not, everything you do is a reflection of your relationship with the truth: the clothes you choose, the texts you send, the friends you have, your posts on social media, and what you see when you look in the mirror. Absolutely everything!

Everything you do is a reflection of your relationship with the truth.

And well, yes, I might sound like the old-fashioned lady you want to run away from before she starts giving you a lecture, but I am writing to you with tears in my eyes. I would have given anything for someone to shake me out of my foolishness!

Even though I identified as a Christian, postmodernism ran through my veins. Do you want to know how this thirteen-letter word works? I used to think that if what other people said about God and the Bible made me feel good, then it must be true—without even checking it firsthand in Scripture. I approached the Bible with the idea that I was the center of God's plan, and I used verses—without taking their context into account—to claim what God had in store for me. My perceptions and my points of view counted for more than the absolute truth of His Word.

That is how I built my own definition of what truth was. If it worked and made me feel good, then it was true for me. If I found a Bible verse that supported what I was doing, then it was right.

For example, this advice was repeated to me often: "If you want to be someone in life, you must work and not depend on anyone." I connected that with what I found in my deceitful heart, which drove me toward ambition. Then I reconciled all that with an idea that seemed biblical to me, such as "The Lord will make you the head and not the tail," and boom! I had created "my truth" about how success should work for a woman.

Of course, this wasn't something that happened consciously. It was just that the pieces I had inside me resulted in the "truths" that defined me.

My lack of appreciation for motherhood originated in the idea that God had called me to do big things, and that if others could help me with that kind of "mundane" thing, then I could focus on empowering myself to pursue greatness and blah, blah, blah. During some of my teenage years, I dressed so others would see me as an evangelical without understanding that, in reality, I was doing it to make myself stand out, so others would notice my "dedication." Later, I found myself using more provocative clothing because, ultimately, no one could judge me. What a fool!

I AM THE TRUTH

—Jesus

JOHN 14:6

Do you see how my thoughts informed my decisions? And this did not happen overnight. Just exposing myself to lies, like taking little sips, was slowly poisoning me. Like those occasions when—while flipping through the pages of a magazine in doctors' waiting rooms—I exposed myself to lies about sex. Or watching a commercial encouraging me to think that I deserved everything or a movie that subtly inspired me to feel compassion for a woman who "had reasons" to be unfaithful to her husband. Unfortunately, I did not expose myself to the lies just in the media but also in Christian circles where the truth of the Word of God did not prevail.

Do you see? These are the same thoughts that have repeated throughout history. The lies that infiltrate our hearts and promise to make us feel good. Let's go over the list, and this time mark the ones you've found yourself thinking:

- I define my own truth!
- Don't try to define me by your personal truth!
- No one can judge me.
- The truth is what works for me or makes me feel good.
- The truth is what I have been taught.
- You offend me if you do not accept and respect my truth.
- The truth is relative. Everyone can decide the truth that is "right" for them.
- The truth is subjective. Everyone has the right to define it according to their experience or reasoning.

These thoughts pass silently through our minds, but our actions display their effects. And they all come from the same source: the deceitful words that Satan spoke to the woman. Look at how they are manifested in our times:

- *"Did God really say that?"* His authority is not as radical as you might think. You don't have to take everything literally. Maybe He said this for the people in ancient times. Open your mind, listen to what others think, and make your own conclusions.
- *"You won't die."* Don't exaggerate! Do you really think that such a good God would send you to hell for something so simple? Follow your heart and do what seems right to you. Things will turn out fine.
- *"You will be like God."* Just wait and see how good it feels when you empower yourself and live according to your personal truth. Be faithful to yourself and take control of your life.

This is the central message of deceit: "Ignore the truth. Jump on the roller coaster of your own desires and decisions. Enjoy the intensity and adrenaline of sin, and you will find that at the end of the ride, you will be safe and without a scratch." I have bought this lie more times than I'd like to admit, and what has driven me is my delight in the sin, my poor discernment, and my lack of love for the truth.

The Truth Is a Person

In this complicated mess, how can we define the truth? If, unlike Pilate, we leave cynicism behind and we ask with a pure heart, what would the answer be?

The answer is as simple as it is profound.

Truth is consistent with the mind, will, character, glory, and being of God. Even more to the point: Truth is the self-expression of God.[2]

All truth flows from the nature of God. His truth stands forever (Isaiah 40:8; 1 Peter 1:25). His Word is the truth (Psalm 119:160; John 17:17), and Jesus is the visible manifestation of that truth (Colossians 1:15). He is the truth incarnate (John 1:14). Any attempt to define truth without seeking Him and His Word as a reference point will end in error.

Because truth is the self-expression of God, Jesus told Pilate that his purpose was to testify to the truth (John 18:37). He is the path to return to the garden we were cast out of. He is the truth that frees us from the power of lies. He is the life that saves us from death (14:6). He is the light that illuminates our darkness (8:12). Jesus is the truth incarnate that Pilate did not recognize.

This is not a mere philosophical subject. The truth is a person and His name is Christ. The truth of God is absolute. It does not come in half measures, nor does it allow for any negotiation. This is why we reject it, because it is absolute. It does not allow any reasoning that may excuse our sin. It places us either in the light or in the darkness.

The truth is a person and His name is Christ.

God's truth is not passive but rather calls us to action. With Jesus, it is all or nothing. That is how profound His truth is.

> Then he said to the crowd, "If any of you wants to be my follower, you must give up your own way, take up your cross daily, and follow me." (Luke 9:23)

> If you try to hang on to your life, you will lose it. But if you give up your life for my sake and for the sake of the Good News, you will save it. And what do you benefit if you gain the whole world but lose your own soul? (Mark 8:35–36)

Do you see why it is easier to run from the truth? Because we cannot play with it. It not only exposes our sin but also requires everything from us. The seduction of the world, of our sinful desires, and of Satan are much easier because they invite us to give free rein to our passions. And it may seem much more appealing to go with the flow that urges us to live for ourselves and put ourselves on the thrones of our lives. Who wouldn't want to live by their own rules? The only problem is that true life is not found there. It is only an illusion of pleasure, like fireworks that light up but then vanish in the blink of an eye.

And you might think, like I did and like Jesus's disciples did, "These are really tough words! The way of truth is radical!"

> Many of his disciples said, "This is very hard to understand. How can anyone accept it?" (John 6:60)

But no matter how narrow the door looks (Matthew 7:13–14), do not run from the truth, because eternal life is only in Jesus.

> At this point many of his disciples turned away and deserted him. Then Jesus turned to the Twelve and asked, "Are you also going to leave?"
>
> Simon Peter replied, "Lord, to whom would we go? You have the words that give eternal life. We believe, and we know you are the Holy One of God." (verses 66–69)

It is my prayer that you may be able to say, like Simon Peter, "To whom would we go? You have the words that give eternal life." It is in the person of Christ, in His work on our behalf, in His promises, and in His Word, that we find the truth.

Whether you are exploring the faith, you are a new believer, or—like me—you have been on this path for years, I invite you to assume that you do not know everything. Set your own reasoning down on the table. Listen to Christ and ask God to open your eyes to the truth of His Word, for His Holy Spirit to guide you to the whole truth and conquer any rebellion that may arise against His authority. Then you will see the freedom that can be found when we give ourselves over to the truth!

> You will know the truth, and the truth will set you free. (8:32)

I pray that the Holy Spirit gives you a heart on fire for His truth, a deep thirst for the living water, and a renewed passion for His Word. I invite you to take a moment to present yourself before the Lord.

Make It Personal

- How would you define *truth* in your own words?
- Do your actions reflect the thinking of the world or the truth of God's Word?
- While you were reading this chapter, did you identify any lies that you have believed?
- Ask the Lord to reveal the lies you have stored in your heart throughout this journey. Pray the words of Psalm 139:23–24: "Search me, O God, and know my heart; test me and know my anxious thoughts. Point out anything in me that offends you, and lead me along the path of everlasting life."
- Ask the Lord to grant you sincere repentance and transform your mind with the truth.

TWO

How Will the Truth Change Me?

BETSY GÓMEZ

"Here is the Bible. Show me where it says that." These words fell on us like a bucket of cold water in the middle of the night. We were eating dinner at the house of some really close friends, and it was there that we met Lázaro, the first person to challenge our convictions. My husband loves debating issues of faith—with much passion. We both enjoy the conversations, and we always had a biblical answer—or at least we thought so. Our passion for defending our points of view made us appear very convincing, and we won the argument in most cases.

But this night was different. Lázaro's challenge disarmed us. He left us in a silence revealing that we had no idea where we had gotten that belief we considered biblical and fiercely defended. You cannot imagine how clueless we felt (though we didn't show it because we wanted to win the argument). But he did know where to find the passage we were referring to.

Reading it carefully was enough to convince us that, in reality, it said the opposite of what we had been thinking. All it took was opening the Bible and reading the entire chapter instead of focusing on a single verse. We could not believe what we were seeing. Our world was turned upside down!

We went home that night with a lot of questions. I wish I could tell you that we were new believers and that we didn't know much, but my husband and I had been serving as youth leaders in the church for years. Although we both grew up in Christian contexts and loved God, we were holding on to many wrong convictions that we learned from others. Unlike the people in Berea, who respectfully received the teaching but examined everything in the light of the

Scriptures in order to confirm whether it was true (Acts 17:10–11), we took everything for granted and did not verify whether anything we were learning was in line with the Word of God and, even worse, we repeated these things to others.

If it was logical, if it said something impressive, if it made us feel good and seemed biblical or spiritual, then we considered it the truth.

Yes, we knew and believed we were sinners and that Jesus had died on the cross to save us from our sins, but we piled on a mountain of theories and practices that did not come from the Word of God.

God, in His grace, used Lázaro—who is a great friend today—so that we would realize that professing Christ as Lord and Savior requires an absolute submission to the authority of His Word.

From that moment, God brought a revival into our lives, and everything—absolutely everything—changed. That is the effect of the truth.

Professing Christ as Lord and Savior requires an absolute submission to the authority of His Word.

For the first time, we were ready to put our convictions aside so that the Word of God could transform our understanding (Romans 12:1–2). The cost of submitting ourselves to His authority was high, but nothing could compare with the joy we felt from consuming the truth (Jeremiah 15:16; Philippians 3:8). We were like newborn babies, hungry to know more about God (1 Peter 2:2)!

Everything changed. Christian life seemed more colorful, and our hearts were overflowing with fullness. The truth transformed my way of seeing God and how I approached Him. It replaced the lies I had believed about what it meant to be a woman and reshaped my emotions. It shifted my priorities and revolutionized my whole way of living.

When I share this with young people, they often ask me, "How did you change? How do I know if my life isn't shaped by the truth? What do I have to do to change?"

I wish I could give you three simple steps to help you put your life in order. If only I could jump out of the pages to give you a quick fix. But if I did, I would be leading you down a path of shallow moralism.

Before we dive into how life under the authority of the Word of God works, we need to pass Go. (Ever played Monopoly?) To get to a starting point so we can see where everything truly comes from. The starting point in your journey to shape your life by the truth is the gospel because the work of Christ is the only gateway to the transformation that you're longing for.

Bad News

Imagine someone tells you, "We've got some bad news and good news. Which would you like to hear first?" How would you answer? I have always chosen the bad news first, in the hope that the good news would ease the problem. But I admit that when it came to the gospel, I made an exception, and I wanted only the good news.

I was fine knowing that Christ died for my sins and that He had a wonderful plan for me. I knew I was a sinner and needed help, but I didn't understand the reality of my condition. Much less understand the greatness of the holiness of God or the magnitude of my rebellion against this God who condemns sin. The bad news that I learned didn't seem to be so dreadful.

I didn't think of myself as bad because I considered myself a church girl—until the Word of God, like a mirror, showed me the truth. I couldn't believe what it revealed. I thought I was going to see a Caribbean version of Sleeping Beauty, but the mirror showed me something else. It showed that I was dead.

Not understanding the depth of my awful condition kept me from appreciating the good news of the gospel. To truly value what Christ did for us, we first need to see the reality of who we are with open eyes. So we must take a look at the dark side and see how the fall of Adam and Eve in Eden broke the communion between God and humankind and damaged everything.

Look at this portrait of our condition without Christ, brought to us by the Word of God (and don't rush through the verses; take the time to find them and read them in your Bible).

- We are living apart from God (Ephesians 2:12; Romans 3:23).
- We are enemies of God (Colossians 1:21; Romans 5:10).
- We are daughters of disobedience (Ephesians 2:1–2).
- We are to delight in and follow the way of this world (Ephesians 2:3).
- We are children of wrath (Ephesians 2:3).
- We are incapable of seeking God and doing good (Psalm 14:3; Romans 3:10).
- We are blind and cannot see the light of the gospel (2 Corinthians 4:3–4).
- We are dead because of our offenses and sins (Colossians 2:13; Ephesians 2:5).

How awful! This description defines not only the worst of criminals but also the condition of every human being, and we are no exception. Whether we think that we have never messed up or that we are the biggest sinners in history, because of our sin, the only thing we deserve is eternal condemnation and separation from the glory of God (Romans 3:23). In Adam, our sin made us enemies of God—yes, you read that right—enemies! Enemies of the king and creator of everything that exists.

But there is something even darker. Without Christ, we were the object of God's wrath. Can you imagine the force of the wrath of an omnipotent God? Even worse, no matter how hard we tried, we were incapable of doing anything good enough to earn God's approval. So of course there was no way to meet His standard. We weren't able to attain the justice and holiness that God demands. Our sin turned all our works into filthy rags (Isaiah 64:6). How depressing!

Do you see how dreadful our reality was? A dead person cannot do anything for themselves. We did not need any kind of medicine; we needed a resurrection.

Good News!

Good news please! In the midst of the darkness that sin brought upon humanity, God promised that One would come who would destroy the power of death (Genesis 3:15)—One better than Adam, who would come to save us from our horrendous condition and the consequences we deserved. (What a relief!) And throughout the Scriptures, we see how God lifted up men who pointed to this Savior. Christ is the culmination of the promise of God! He is the truth incarnate, who came to rescue us from the abyss that separated us from God.

From Genesis to Revelation, God's revealed plan is Christ. Every character in the Bible—the ones you probably learned about in Sunday school or in Christian movies—is only a shadow of the best and truest. I love how Pastor Tim Keller summed up how everything points to Him.

- There is a true and better Adam, who passed the test in the garden and whose obedience is granted to us. . . .
- There is a true and better Abraham, who answered the call of God to leave everything behind and who went out into the void to form a new people of God.
- There is a true and better Isaac. The son of laughter, of grace, who was not only offered by his father on the mountain but was truly sacrificed for us. . . .

Born again THROUGH THE **Word of God**

1 PETER 1:23

- There is a true and better Joseph, who, at the right hand of the King, forgives those who betrayed and sold him and uses his new power to save them.
- There is a true and better Moses, who stepped into the breach between the people and the Lord and is the mediator of a new covenant. . . .
- There is a true and better David, whose victory is turned into the victory of the people, even though they didn't lift a stone. . . .
- There is a true and better Passover lamb: innocent, perfect, defenseless, sacrificed so that the angel of death might pass by.
- He is the true temple, the true prophet, priest and king, the true lamb and sacrifice, the true light, and the true bread.[1]

Do you see how our perspective changes when we see how the whole Bible points to Christ?

The gospel is the culmination of the promise of salvation. It is the good news that in Christ, God sent the solution to the problem of our sin.

What wonderful news! God sent His Son to save us from all condemnation. Jesus came down from His throne and took the form of a servant, similar to us.

The gospel is the good news that in Christ, God sent the solution to the problem of our sin.

He lived a perfect life and obeyed God in everything—something that neither you nor I will ever be able to achieve. He followed the 613 laws of the Old Testament. (Yes, you read that correctly, 613!) And being innocent, He took the punishment we deserve for our sins. The Just One went to the cross for our wrongs and died as we should have.

But the story does not end there.

The good news is truly very good because He did not remain in the tomb.

He rose and conquered the power of death. His resurrection is the guarantee that God accepted His sacrifice in our place and granted Him victory over every power.

Jesus lived, died, and rose in our place.

The truth of the gospel not only restores our relationship with God on this earth but also gives us a hope that extends beyond this world. Christ will return and restore all things. Then there will be no more death, suffering, or sin, only joy in His presence for all eternity. The happy ending that we all wish for!

How Does the Truth of the Gospel Transform Me?

When we see the truth about our awful condition and the beautiful work of Christ in saving us, all the lies we have believed regarding the gospel disappear. Have you identified any? I have.

I am free from the misconception that the gospel is a list of rules I have to follow to earn my salvation or that it's merely to create a better version of myself. It's not about the prosperity I can gain in this world. It's not just about repeating a prayer on my knees at an altar. I was dead, unable to do anything by myself, and was resurrected by the one who conquered death!

The gospel places me at the foot of the cross because I remember that there is absolutely nothing I can do to deserve or earn such a great salvation. It crushes my pride and humbles me, leading me to recognize that only God is worthy of glory. The gospel helps me to understand that someone without life cannot love, that I love Him now simply because He loved me first (1 John 4:19). It reminds me that my love for Christ is a response to the work He began in me.

Everything Changes

Do you get it? The truth of the gospel transforms absolutely everything! It changes our desires and priorities; it changes our hearts. It moves us out of the darkness into the light, from error to truth, from death to life.

However, if we are honest, we must admit that there are times when it is not easy to connect the gospel with our everyday lives. It was much easier for me to settle for the superficiality that defined the young women of my generation than to ground my identity in these profound truths.

For many years, I was like a weak tree in a hurricane because I did not feed my roots with the truth spoken about me in God's Word.

Do you know what helped me stand firm when my emotions wanted to deceive me or the pressure of the world was screaming lies about my worth or purpose? Remembering what Christ did, what I am in Him, and all the blessings that He granted me through His salvation.

This is totally countercultural! I want to challenge you to fill your mind with these truths, even if they sound like a Sunday sermon to you. Do you know why? Because I don't want you to be like an old woman on her deathbed who realizes that, long ago, a relative had left her a millionaire's inheritance and she lived in poverty her whole life out of ignorance. Believing the truth gives you an abundant life!

How Will You Respond?

Once we've recognized the bad news of our condition and learned the good news of Christ's work, the next question is, How should we respond?

The only way to respond to this good news is by faith. There is no YouTube tutorial. There is no series of steps or shortcuts.

> By grace you have been saved through faith; and this is not your own doing, it is the gift of God—not because of works, lest any man should boast. (Ephesians 2:8–9 RSV)

We believe in the gospel by faith, and faith is a gift from God; it is a change of heart. God removes our dead hearts, our hearts of stone, and gives us new hearts that now live for God (Ezekiel 36:26). This is the greatest and most wonderful miracle of all! What a great mystery!

If by now you have realized that you need this change of heart, I want to invite you to pause in order to come before God in repentance. Acknowledge your inability to save yourself and ask Him to give you eyes to see Christ as your Savior. Put all your trust in His sacrifice and power to give you a new life in Him. When God gives us the faith to believe in Christ, the Holy Spirit begins to dwell inside us and enables us to live according to His will. Isn't it incredible, that God, Creator of heaven and earth, would come to dwell in us?

When God gives us the faith to believe in Christ, the Holy Spirit begins to dwell inside us and enables us to live according to His will.

If you are now a daughter of God, consider joining in the apostle Paul's plea:

> I urge you, brothers and sisters, in view of God's mercy [*for all that Christ has done on your behalf*], to offer your

> bodies as a living sacrifice, holy and pleasing to God—this is your true and proper worship [*this is the logical response to such mercy*]. Do not conform to the pattern of this world [*don't imitate the behaviors of this world or be shaped by its patterns*], but be transformed by the renewing of your mind [*let the truth of God's Word renew your mind and transform your actions*]. Then you will be able to test and approve [*so that you will know and love*] what God's will is—his good, pleasing and perfect will. (Romans 12:1–2 NIV)

Live in the Light of the Truth

You Belong to a New Kingdom

In Christ, you are not a slave to sin! In the past, sin commanded us, and we obeyed. We had no choice but to live chained to sin, tripping up on it again and again.

But Christ broke those chains. We are no longer slaves under the control of sin because the same power that resurrected Him from the dead enables us to please God and live in freedom (John 8:36; Romans 8:11). You no longer need to live bound to that sin that secretly robs you of freedom.

You are free!

Christ paid the price of our freedom with His blood. We are no longer slaves (Ephesians 1:7).

You Belong to a New Family

Sin left us wounded, orphaned, helpless, and unprotected. That's why most young women do whatever they need in order to feel that they belong to something or someone. However, we do not have to chase after an illusion of refuge. God showed His great love for us by choosing us from before the beginning of the world to be His through His Son (Ephesians 1:4–6).

God saved us and adopted us as daughters. He is our Father, and in Him we have everything we need. In Christ, we have been adopted into the family of God (John 1:12). Now the blessings that Christ enjoys as the Son of God are ours because of His obedience on our behalf. We are coheirs with Christ (Romans 8:17; Galatians 4:7)!

We do not have to beg for the crumbs the world offers. We do not have to seek acceptance anywhere else. We have a place at the table of our Father, the King of Kings. What could be better?

There Are More Blessings!

Jesus did not just die for us. He also lived a perfect life in our place and, by resurrecting, offered us the greatest exchange there could be. He took our sin-stained garments and gave us His robes of righteousness. A complete transformation! He dressed us in the blessings of His perfect life, death, and resurrection (Isaiah 61:10; Revelation 3:4).

We do not have to beg for the crumbs the world offers. We have a place at the table of our Father, the King of Kings.

We are clothed in the garments of Christ's justice and perfection, twenty-four hours a day, seven days a week (2 Corinthians 5:21; 1 John 2:1).

We are free from the exhaustion of trying to please God in order to earn His favor, because all the approval that Christ earned is now ours (Romans 5:1). He erased the D from our report card and inserted the A+ that He had earned. Wonderful! Christ met the standard. He declares us justified.

We have been separated for God. It's awesome to know that the holiness of Christ is now our identities and also our callings. When God looks at you, do you know what He sees? The holiness of Christ! Best of all, He does not leave us as we are. He has promised to make us more like Him every day. Is that not great?

When you feel discouraged by your weakness, you can cling to this promise: God is shaping the image of Christ in you.

We are loved and accepted. Christ bore all the wrath of God that weighed down on us (Hebrews 2:17; John 3:36). God isn't angry with us! His perfect sacrifice appeased all the wrath that weighed down on our shoulders. Now, instead of fleeing from Him, we can run confidently to His throne, knowing that we will receive the grace and aid we need (Hebrews 4:16).

Christ relieved us of the label that says "Guilty, unjust, slave, orphan, enemy, and dead in sin" and gave us one that says "Free, just, adopted, daughter, risen in Christ."

We have an identity and a purpose! We belong exclusively to God to share the goodness that has taken us out of darkness and brought us into His wonderful light (1 Peter 2:9).

I feel like my head is going to explode! These are truths we need to believe and process because they are essential to grounding ourselves in Christ.

The world will shout lies at you about your identity. They will probably come from the voices of people you admire or sources that seem trustworthy. They will feel like strong gusts of wind, but none of them will knock you down if you stand firm in the truth of what Christ did for you.

Take a moment to meditate on everything Christ has done for you, and ask Him to increase your awe of His mercy and help you align your life with the truth as a result. Pray to be convicted of sin in the areas where you need to repent, and ask Him to help you live in light of the identity He has provided for you. The gospel is the engine that drives everything that we do for God!

Make It Personal

- Do the ideas you consume pass through the filter of the Word of God, or do you rely on your own logic?
- Are you willing to put your convictions aside and submit yourself to the authority of the Word of God?
- Why is the gospel the starting point of our journey to the truth?
- Read Romans 12:1–2. How can you present your life as an offering to God for what He has done for you? In what practical ways can you avoid copying the behavior and ways of this world in your everyday life?

THREE

Where Can the Truth Be Found?

ERIN DAVIS

It was a mean girl who led me to Jesus. I had a hard day at school. A friend who had turned into a frenemy was talking behind my back, spreading rumors that were not true and made me feel miserable inside. As I collapsed onto my bed and sobbed into my pillow, suddenly a small pink Bible called to me from the bookshelf. It was not an audible sound, but a subtle heart tug toward the Word of God I had never felt before.

At that moment, if you had asked me, "Where is the truth?" I would have stared at you, disconcerted, with my eyes full of tears. I was not a Christian yet. I couldn't tell the difference between Psalms and Proverbs. I was incapable of explaining the gospel. I had no idea how the Word of God was going to transform me. I only knew that I needed advice, and I thought the Bible could be a good resource.

Discovering what was true—about God, about me, and about the world around me—seemed like an impossible mission. I didn't know where to look. Until the truth came looking for me.

Enough about me. Let's talk about you. Where do you seek the truth?

- Are you constantly looking at social media, trying to discover the truth about the world around you?
- Do you trust that your feelings will tell you what is true?
- Do you lean on other people to show you the truth about who you are?

- Do you depend on your friends to help you know what you believe?

If you want to know the truth but aren't sure where to look in order to find it, you've come to the right place. No mean girls here! I am cheering for you with open arms and a big smile. I am eager to help you discover the answer to the question, Where is the truth? Are you ready? Let's go!

THE. WORD. WAS. GOD!

Find John 1:1 in your Bible. Listen to how the apostle John described the beginning of everything.

> In the beginning the Word already existed.
> The Word was with God,
> and the Word was God.

You may already know this passage. At first glance, it may seem like a simple idea. But sometimes when things seem familiar, we read them quickly and forget to pay attention. This single sentence, in reality, is packed with mind-blowing truth. Let's break it down.

"In the beginning the Word already existed."

Q: When did the Word come into existence?

A: In the beginning.

The Bible you use hasn't always existed. The words it contains were written by men who had not yet been born at the beginning of time. And the books of the Bible were compiled much later. So how can we be sure that the Word was with God since the beginning of everything? Let's go back to what the final line says in order to find out.

"The Word was God."

Do you mind if I rewrite it in Erin's style? The. Word. Was. God! (This is so good!)

The Word is not just a book.

It is not merely a collection of books.

It is not something that we wrap in a pink cover and leave on a shelf.

The Word is a person. That person is Jesus! Look at other passages of the Scriptures that describe Him this way.

> The Word became human and made his home among us. He was full of unfailing love and faithfulness. And we

> have seen his glory, the glory of the Father's one and only Son. (verse 14)

> He wore a robe dipped in blood, and his title was the Word of God. (Revelation 19:13)

Jesus is the Word of God, but how does this help us know the truth? Listen to what He said in His prayer for us in John 17:17.

> Make them holy by your truth; teach them your word, which is truth.

Let's connect the dots.

God's Word Is Truth

Christians believe the Bible is not only *true* but the source of all truth. The Bible is a deep well. When we ask ourselves what's true about ourselves or about the world around us, we can cast our buckets into the Word of God, and every time we do it, we bring up profound truth from this well.

Jesus Is the Word

Whether you're a high school girl with a broken heart or a much older woman (ahem) like me who is trying to live for what she was created for, we are all seeking the truth. As you read in the earlier chapters, we can begin to find answers only when we approach the person of Jesus.

The Sixty-Six-Piece Puzzle

As we wrestle with the question, Where is the truth? it's likely that you have figured out the short answer by now: the Bible. But sometimes we forget, right? Like the sinners that we are, we tend to give way to the natural impulse to seek truth elsewhere. We must resist this impulse. Let's think about why God gave us His Word by using the imagery of a puzzle.

A rainy day spent assembling a puzzle sounds like my idea of heaven. It fascinates me to empty the box of pieces onto a table and then, slowly and meticulously, put them together until they form a complete picture.

The Bible is my favorite puzzle. Each one of the sixty-six books of the Old and New Testaments is a piece. As we read them, study them, and memorize them, we are turning over a piece of the puzzle. And what is the picture that we are putting together? The image of God.

The purpose of the Bible is to reveal who God is. Wait. Let me say it again. The purpose of the Bible is to reveal who God is.

The Bible is not simply a history book. It is not a self-help book to create better human beings. God has given us His Word so that we can know who He is.

When we skip parts of the Bible, maybe only sticking to the parts we understand, we lose pieces of the puzzle. We're probably getting an incomplete picture of who God is. Since God is the source of the truth, this may lead us to a tenuous or erroneous understanding of the truth.

The Bible is not simply a history book. It is not a self-help book. God has given us His Word so that we can know who He is.

We Can Know God

God is huge! He is mysterious. We will never understand everything about Him on this side of heaven. But He has not hidden Himself from us. He calls us to know Him. This means He invites us to know His truth.

Listen.

> "They will not need to teach their neighbors, nor will they need to teach their relatives, saying, 'You should know the Lord.' For everyone, from the least to the greatest, will know me already," says the Lord. (Jeremiah 31:34)
>
> Be still, and know that I am God! (Psalm 46:10)
>
> I love all who love me.
> Those who search will surely find me.
> (Proverbs 8:17)

This message echoes throughout the Scriptures: "My people can know Me. My people can know Me. My people can know me."

We can know God! How? Through His Word. And since God is the source of all truth, the more we know Him, the more we are rooted and grounded in the Word. While you're reading these words, it may be that you're nodding your head. It may be that you are thinking, "Yes! The Word of God is the truth!" Or, "I want to know God through His Word."

Or maybe you are more like I was when I first started reading the Bible. Maybe you don't understand much of what you are reading yet. Maybe you still have more questions than answers, but in your search for the truth, you feel an urge to open your Bible and hear what God says.

Wherever you are on that spectrum, we all need frequent reminders to open our Bibles when we are seeking the truth. And as we commit to opening our Bibles daily, we will be transformed little by little, because the more we know the character of God, the more we can repattern our lives to be like His.

The Word of God is the road map that shows us who we were made to be. Listen to the words of the prophet Isaiah as written in Isaiah 43:6–7:

> I will say to the north and south,
> "Bring my sons and daughters back to Israel
> from the distant corners of the earth.
> Bring all who claim me as their God,
> for I have made them for my glory.
> It was I who created them."

Take your Bible and reread this passage. Underline verse 7.

This verse addresses the most fundamental question that we may ask ourselves: "Why do I exist?" The answer is in this passage, as if it were staring us in the face. We were made to give glory to God. Genesis 1:27 tells us how this is possible: by being the bearers of His image, by being like Him.

How can we expect to be like God if we don't know Him? The more you see His character through His Word, the more you will be able to reflect His image and give Him glory.

Don't you want to run to the truth of the Word of God? Here are some reasons why you need to make reading the Bible your priority.

The Bible Is a Way to Talk to God and Hear His Voice

Wouldn't you like to sit down for coffee with God and hear His heart? Well, you can! Or something like that . . . I'm afraid that on this side of heaven, we can't actually have a coffee with God. (But I obviously hope there is coffee in heaven!) But you can listen to God through His Word.

Did you know that 2 Timothy 3:16 says that *all* the Scriptures are inspired by God? They are not only the ideas of God or things we think God would say to us.

In 1 Thessalonians 2:13, Paul put it this way: "We never stop thanking God that when you received his message from us, you didn't think of our words *as mere human ideas*. You accepted what we said *as the very word of God*—which, of course, it is. And this word continues to work in you who believe."

Yes, humans played a part in the written record of the Bible, but Paul reminded us that it isn't the words of humankind, but rather the definitive Word of God. It is the thoughts of God expressed in His own Words. If you wish to know God, the Bible is a great way to do so!

The Bible Is a Good Teacher

How can we study outside of church?

The answer is—yes, you've guessed it—by reading the Bible!

In 2 Timothy 3:16, we are told that all the Scriptures are useful for teaching and correcting in justice. Romans 15:4 says that the Word was written for our instruction.

The best place to learn about God is not through our feelings. It is not through what other people tell us about God. It is not even through excellent books about God. In the study of God, the Bible is our best teacher.

The Bible Is Alive

Hebrews 4:12 tells us that the Word of God is "alive and powerful."

My Bible does not breathe. It does not have a beating heart. I have not noticed it doing jumping jacks lately. What is the meaning of this passage when it describes the Bible as alive and powerful?

It means that the Bible is more than a book. The words of the Bible do not change, but their effects on us do. It is the only written book that can be relevant at every stage of our lives and that presents us with truth to suit every need.

The Bible Is a Good Surgeon

The rest of Hebrews 4:12 tells us that the Word of God is "sharper than the sharpest two-edged sword, cutting between soul and spirit, between joint and marrow. It exposes our innermost thoughts and desires."

This verse describes the Bible as a very sharp sword.

The Word does more than simply entertain us, encourage us, or inform us. When we read the Bible, it works in parts of our being that must submit to God, leaving us healthier, with a holier heart and life.

IN THE BEGINNING

the Word

ALREADY EXISTED.

The Word

was with God,

AND

the Word

was God.

JOHN 1:1

If there is trash in your life that shouldn't be there (hint: we all have it), you need the Bible to do its work.

The Bible Encourages Us

Romans 15:4 says, "Such things were written in the Scriptures long ago to teach us. And the Scriptures give us hope and encouragement as we wait patiently for God's promises to be fulfilled."

The Bible is designed to be a great source of encouragement and hope. Not all the passages in the Bible encourage us, but the principal ideas of the Bible—that God loves us, He wants to forgive us, He is preparing a place for us, and in time He will defeat everything that afflicts us—should comfort and inspire us.

Do you need encouragement? Open your Bible.

The Bible Works Like a Magnifying Glass

In addition to assuring us that the Bible is inspired by God and useful for teaching, 2 Timothy 3:16 tells us that it is useful for correcting. This is an elegant way of saying that it puts our sin under a magnifying glass.

I am not very good at seeing my own sin. It's very easy to justify myself, invent excuses, and compare. However, sin (including the sin that I don't see) works like acid, eating away at my being. If it is not taken away, sin can end up destroying me. So I'm thankful that the Bible has the power to bring my sin into the light, even the sin that is hard for me to see.

The Bible Is a Belt

In 1 Peter 1:13, we read, "Gird up your minds, be sober, set your hope fully upon the grace that is coming to you at the revelation of Jesus Christ" (RSV).

When was the last time you used the expression "gird up your minds" in a sentence? It's not a frequently used phrase, but the image it presents is the idea of fastening our clothes with belts, of preparing ourselves for action, of having everything ready and set. The function of a belt is to secure, hold, and enclose.

The Word of God has the power to protect us from enemies we can see and enemies we cannot see. It prepares us to live our lives for Christ no matter what comes. It surrounds us and sustains us when our worlds go into tailspins. It provides secure footing in a broken world.

The Bible Is a Filter

Another word for *screen* is *filter*. The Bible is much more than a list of rules or stories. It can be a filter to see life more clearly. You can take the questions, problems, and worries you have throughout your life and filter them through the Word of God, and you will always find answers.

The Bible Is a Tether

Here is a surprising fact: Most young people from Christian homes end up abandoning their faith. If nothing changes, it is very likely that you will be one of those girls who grew up in the church, listened to the teachings of Jesus, and spent years trying to follow Him, but ultimately decided to take a different path.

The Bible surrounds us and sustains us when our worlds go into tailspins. It provides secure footing in a broken world.

The truth of God has the power to keep you focused on God Himself. Here is the good part: When you know the truth of God, you can take refuge in Him. But if you don't know the Word, if you do not cultivate the habit of regularly studying the truth of God and applying it to your decisions, if you are not "tethered" by what God teaches you throughout the Bible, you will find that you are exposed and insecure.

If you wish to stand firm in the face of the seductions of this world, you need to know, believe, and live the Word of God.

The Truth Is Like a Castle

Amusement park visitors often experience something called "museum feet." This is the general feeling of being lost or exhausted that results from spending time in a big open space. Having museum feet can be a bad experience for people and even cause them to leave the park. But if architects include a large visual landmark, like Cinderella Castle, Spaceship Earth in EPCOT, or Hogwarts at Universal Studios, it is less likely that people will feel overwhelmed.

The Bible works the same way. Life is very expansive. It is easy to feel lost or overwhelmed. At times, each of us wants to throw in the towel. But when we know the truth of God, we are anchored and safe from museum feet. The truth gives us a reference point we can return to when we feel alone, insignificant, or afraid.

The Word of God is like our fairy-tale castle. We can go to it again and again in search of answers. When we feel discouraged, we can go to the Word of God and find hope. When we are afraid, we can go to the Word of God and find peace. When we are confused, we can go to the Word of God and find answers.

This is why Jesus made us this promise: "You are truly my disciples if you remain faithful to my teachings. And you will know the truth, and the truth will set you free" (John 8:31–32).

The truth frees us from living adrift without knowing why we are here. It is an anchor that keeps us standing firm.

Even though a lot of time has passed since a mean girl drove me to open my little pink Bible for the first time, I still ask myself, "Where is the truth?" I ask myself this question every day. What has changed? Now I know the answer!

- God is Truth.
- I can know God!
- He has revealed Himself through His Word.

The truth frees us from living adrift without knowing why we are here. It is an anchor that keeps us standing firm.

The day I opened my Bible for the first time, Jesus had used friendship drama to light a spark in my heart. The embers were strong enough to keep me reading throughout middle school and high school, when I finally gave my life to Christ. Now the truth is a bonfire that consumes my life. Along with the psalmist, I declare, "Your instructions are more valuable to me than millions in gold and silver" (Psalm 119:72). The Word of God has become my greatest treasure. Is it for you too?

Make It Personal

- Is reading the Bible a daily habit for you?
- What is the biggest obstacle that prevents you from reading more of the Word of God?
- When you study the Bible, what question comes up most often? How is it related to Scripture's purpose of revealing who God is?

- Looking back on your life, what has God used to bring you to His Word?
- What step can you take this week to strengthen yourself more in the truth of the Word of God?

PART 2

Standing Firm in the Truth

FOUR

God Has Provided Everything I Need to Stand Firm

AYLÍN MICHELÉN DE MERCK

In the early years of my marriage, Google and I had a great relationship. I would ask, "Google, how do I cook rice?" or "Google, what is the best recipe for chocolate fondue?" And it promptly responded.

The more time passes, the more I use the internet as a mom and homemaker. Pinterest helps me with a thousand and one ideas to organize my home, recipes I can use to feed my family with multiple allergies, and even suggestions for planning my children's birthdays. YouTube helps me with step-by-step tutorials that allow me to do a little bit of everything. A difficult recipe? A Christmas wreath for my front door? How to write a children's book? There it is.

Few things give reassurance to a perfectionist's soul like the certainty of knowing how to do something. Few things cause more fear and anxiety than realizing you don't know something or can't do something important. Trust me—I've been there.

When I was younger, I really hated making mistakes, and I had a strong fear of failure. I wanted to grow up quickly, thinking that age was guaranteed to bring me what I wanted: wisdom, experience, and maturity. "I learn quickly from my mistakes," I told myself, and this gave me confidence. It was like watching a tutorial in reverse. I learned what not to do, and that prepared me to know what to do in similar situations. In the same way, I studied the Word with the goal of knowing what steps I had to take to abide in Christ.

Abide in Christ? What Do You Mean?

Perhaps you've heard a pastor speak about the idea of "abiding in Christ." Or maybe you've read the book of John and come across that phrase a few times. But do you really know what it means?

I used to think that abiding in Christ meant reading my Bible, praying, and obeying God's commands. I thought that remaining in Christ depended on my performance and achievements. I pushed myself hard to please God, but my Christian life felt like a roller coaster of ups and downs. I realized that everything I did wasn't enough, and that made me sad and anxious. That's why I wanted to grow up and learn from my mistakes. I wanted to fail less. However, abiding in Christ was not about always improving and making fewer mistakes. What I needed was to learn to live by faith. How I wish I had understood that when I was your age!

The Lord saved me when I was a child and gave me a genuine desire to do His will. But for many years I tried to live a Christian life in my own strength. I didn't fully understand what it meant to live through faith as a believer. I thought that faith was something we needed at the beginning of the Christian life. I didn't realize it's something I have to rely on every single day.

Living by faith is the key to a Christian life. It is vital to every aspect of our life in Christ. I pray that this chapter helps you understand what this means and how to put it into practice.

To abide in Christ is another way of saying "believe in Christ" (see John 6:56). What do you need to believe?

- Believe that He has made you a branch on His vine, and that He is all that is necessary to supply whatever you need (15:5).
- Believe that He gave His life for you and so calls you a friend.
- Believe that He will protect you to the end (Jude 24).
- Believe that He has freed you to pursue His commands (Psalm 119:32).
- Believe that He gives you the strength to live a life that honors the Father (Philippians 4:13).

Abiding and Being United: They Are Not the Same Thing

As Betsy explained in chapter 2, if you've placed your faith in Christ, you are a living miracle. Christ has united Himself with you in such a way that you and He are one. He is in you, and you are in Him (Galatians 2:20; cf. Ephesians 1).

So, as a grapevine is one with its branches, so we are one with Christ (John 15). This reality never changes. Glory to God!

Because of that, it's important to distinguish between remaining in Christ and our union with Him. John Piper, citing Hudson Taylor, once said, "Our union [with Christ] can never be interrupted, but our enjoyment of it can be."[1]

Let me put it this way. Imagine that one day you start to doubt that you really are your mom and dad's child. You start to search for baby pictures to see if you resemble the baby in those photos. When your mom and dad answer your questions, instead of listening to them with trust, you find yourself evaluating everything that they say to see whether you really believe them. How do you think that would affect your ability to enjoy being with your parents? If during this time of doubt they offer you a present, would you take it with pleasure? Or would you wonder whether they have hidden motives? Do you think you would want to be with them?

That said, your doubts on the matter cannot change the fact that you truly are their daughter. Nothing can change the fact that you have their last name, that they adopted you, or that you carry their genes in your cells. The only thing that has changed is your appreciation for their love, the comfort that you experience from knowing who they are, and therefore who you are.

In the same way, if we have placed our faith in Christ, nothing can separate us from the love of God (Romans 8:39). Our union with Christ is forever. Because of that union, we believe what He says and live in accordance with it. We do not abide for the purpose of preserving the union that Christ has given us. We abide in Him because He has united us with Him. We abide to enjoy who God is and who He is for us in Christ.

Our union with Christ is forever.

In this chapter, we will look at an obstacle that prevents us from abiding in Christ and an important prerequisite for enjoying Him more every moment. First, let's see the obstacle.

Obstacle: Believing in Yourself

I don't know about you, but for many years my hope would rise and fall depending on how I evaluated my performance. When I felt close to God, I was full of joy and confidence. When I felt spiritually cold and saw myself falling into certain temptations, I would get really discouraged, realizing how weak I was.

I thought a lot about *my* performance, *my* desires, *my* emotions. But thinking so much about myself revealed where my faith was placed—in my effort to believe and in what I was capable of doing. My hope went up and down so much because I am not a good object for my faith. No one is.

The only one who has lived and will live a life that satisfies the Father is His beloved Son. If He is the only one who satisfies the Father, nothing is more urgent than taking His life as our own. Praise God that this is possible! He has given us His life (Colossians 3:4), His mind (Philippians 2:5), and His affections (Philippians 1:8). His Spirit is ours and lives in us. His Spirit produces love, joy, peace, patience, kindness, goodness, faithfulness, gentleness, and self-control (Galatians 5:22–23).

So we can have a fruitful life only through Jesus Christ. When I talk about living through faith in Jesus, I am not only referring to faith in what Christ did when He died on the cross, resurrected, and forgave all your sins. I am talking about the faith in who lives in you to produce a life that honors the Father.

Jesus Christ: The Object of Our Faith

Only Jesus Christ deserves to be the object of our faith. The more we know Him, the more our souls are filled with worship and hope. As we come to know what He loves, what He hates, and all that He is, our joy increases because with Him living in us, we can love what He loves, hate what He hates, and choose holiness.

The more we know Him, the more our souls are filled with worship and hope.

Consider how a life of faith in Christ is lived out practically. Maybe you understand that you shouldn't watch certain Netflix shows because of their immoral content. You realize how they affect your thoughts and desires. However, you feel that you can't stop watching them. It feels like they have a strong control over you.

In those moments, you can say, "Yes, I am weak. In my own strength, I'm incapable of stopping myself from watching them. But I am no longer just me. Christ lives in me. He is pure, and He has the power to resist this temptation without sinning. I believe that His power in me gives me the strength to flee from temptation and choose another path. It is no longer just me. I am always, 'I in Christ and Christ in me.'[2] He has not left me."

Or let me give you another example because I want you to see the glorious provision that God has given you in Christ. Maybe you feel an intense envy toward your friends. You hear them talking about their experiences, and you can't be happy for them because you want what they have.

By the grace of God, you recognize that this is your weakness. However, when you live by faith, your focus is not on how weak you are. If you are in Christ, the most important thing about you isn't your weakness but rather Christ's strength. Is Christ envious? No. Does He rejoice with those who rejoice? Yes! Is He generous? Yes, He is! Is He in you? Yes! This means that His ability to rejoice with others and His generosity are yours through faith. Believe that you are not a slave to envy but a slave to Christ.

Where Is Your Faith?

Do you want to know where your faith is? Answer these questions: When you see your sin, what is the tendency of your heart? What do you think about most often? About Christ and His provision? Or about your failures and short-comings?

The answers will help you know where your faith is: in Him or in you.

It is good to recognize your insufficiency. But this is only helpful if it leads you to remain in Christ, to live by faith in Him. Only those who are aware of their inability to live in a way that honors God can truly abide in Him.

Remember: The only life that glorifies God is a life of faith in Christ. When we try to obey by thinking we can do it on our own, we sin.

When we do not live in faith, we sin (Romans 14:23). Hebrews 11:6 makes it clear: "Without faith it is impossible to please [God]" (RSV). When we forget or stop believing that what God says is true, we fail to please our Father. If we do not believe in Him, His words will not remain in us.

The more you believe that He and His words remain in you, the more you will bear fruit that glorifies His name. No matter your own limitations or any weaknesses you face, if you have the Son living in you, you have all that you need. Don't abandon Him, thinking that He is not enough, that you need something more, or that you can be nourished by another source. Abide in Christ.

When our faith is placed in ourselves, recognizing our inability and inadequacy fills us with anxiety. But when our faith is in Him, our greatest joy is discovering more and more the absolute power of Christ to do the will of the Father. As we discover who He is and what He can do, our hope grows without fear. Everything that He is and can do is ours through faith.

Having an awareness of our need for Christ proves we are believing in Him. That is the second lesson my Father has taught me these last few years. Keep going to the next point to understand what I mean.

Prerequisite: Stay Desperate

Only the desperate can abide in Christ. I don't mean hopeless people. I'm referring to those who have an urgent need, a desire that only one thing, or rather one Person, can satisfy.

Christ said, "Just as the living Father sent me and *I live because of the Father*, so the one who feeds on me will live because of me" (John 6:57 NIV). Christ knew He depended on the Father to live on this earth. In a literal sense, the Father alone granted Him power, equipped Him, and comforted Him. That is why Christ often withdrew to be with Him and talk to Him (Luke 5:16). No matter how tired He was or how much agony he experienced, being with His Father was His place of greatest rest and strength (22:41–44). He knew He could do nothing apart from His Father. That, as the Son, He desperately needed His Father. He never forgot this.

Because Christ knew that He lived only through His Father and His Word, two vital characteristics describe His life:

- He fed on the Word.
- He made time alone with His Father.

Given that the life of the Son dwells in us, we have the same need for the Father that His Son here on earth had. When we stop believing in ourselves and believe that we live only through Jesus, we do whatever it takes to be with Him.

Feed on the Word of God

Christ is the blessed one from Psalm 1. He meditated on the law of God by day and by night. It was His delight. He knew the Word perfectly, so he was able to use it to defend Himself against all temptations without sinning (Matthew 4:1–11). He knew all the promises of the Old Testament (Luke 24:27). Christ quoted Moses and the prophets when He taught. He knew that, as the Son of God, He could live only by every word that came from the mouth of God (Matthew 4:4).

We, too, are children. As such, the only word that can feed us is the one that comes from the mouth of God. We abide in His Word when we believe that it is the only source of life (John 6:63).

Truthfully, many times we believe that other things give us life. Are we sad? We want to speak with a friend. Do we feel anxious? We eat half a pan of brownies. Are we happy? We post it on Instagram. Are we depressed? We look for something on Netflix to distract us.

But what would happen if we truly believed that only His Word gives us life? How would that change our daily decisions?

I want to give you some practical ideas for how you can feed yourself daily with the Word of God:

- Read the Bible before grabbing your phone to check social media.
- If you don't have much time in the mornings to study a passage, read a psalm or proverb.
- As you get ready for school, listen to the Bible on audio.
- Dedicate time on weekdays to memorizing a passage of Scripture and on weekends to reading or studying a book of the Bible in depth.
- Set a reminder and read a short book of the New Testament (such as Colossians, Ephesians, 1 Peter, or 1 John). Clock how long it takes you. (Probably no more than twenty minutes.)

Remember, we don't read the Bible to stay united with Christ. We are permanently united with Him through faith. And just as we live only by Him, so we also need Him to feed us with His Word.

We abide in His Word when we believe that it is the only source of life.

Set Aside Some Alone Time with Your Father

As I said before, Christ sought every possible opportunity to be with His Father and talk with Him. Sometimes He even sacrificed sleep for this purpose.

Christ's life of prayer amazes me. Take note of some moments He prayed:

- He prayed when He was baptized (Luke 3:21).
- Sometimes He prayed alone, in the company of His disciples, or in the middle of a crowd (Mark 1:35; John 17).
- Sometimes He spent the entire night praying (Luke 6:12).
- He prayed to bless children (Matthew 19:13–15).
- He prayed before making crucial decisions, such as choosing His disciples (Luke 6:12–13).
- He prayed before He raised Lazarus from the dead (John 11:41–42).
- He prayed while He was in agony (Luke 22:42).

- He prayed as He died (Luke 23:34; Matthew 27:46).
- After the resurrection, He blessed the bread and His disciples (Luke 24:13–49).

Christ sometimes prayed in silence. There were occasions His prayers were cried aloud to God. Sometimes His prayers were short. Other times they were very long.

If you want to grow in your prayer life, I invite you to study the prayer life of Jesus. His life is your life. He is more than just an example for you. He is your holiness. The more familiar you are with how Christ prayed, the more you will be transformed to be able to pray as He prayed (2 Corinthians 3:18).

Some practical ideas for how you can grow in your prayer life:

- Write down your prayers.
- Use the acrostic ACTS (adoration, confession, thanksgiving, and supplication).
- Accept the Holy Spirit's invitations to pray. If He brings a person to mind, pray for them. If there is worry that won't leave you, use it as an opportunity to speak with your Father.
- Use a prayer calendar. For example, on Mondays pray for your parents and siblings, on Tuesdays for your pastors and teachers, on Wednesdays for your unsaved family members, and so on.
- Pray using Bible verses. Take a passage from the Scriptures and use the verses to guide your prayer. For example, use Colossians 1:9–12 to pray for your mom: "Father, I give you thanks that you have allowed my mom to share in the inheritance of the believers in the light. I pray that she will be full of knowledge of Your will, and that You will mold her life, drawing her closer to You each day. You know her roles as a wife, mother, church member, and employee. Show her Your will in each of these areas so she can go through life in a way that is worthy of You, bearing fruit that glorifies Your name."

Christ Is Sufficient

This book deals with many themes that are important and relevant to you: purity, relationships, depression, and anxiety. What do you think when you consider these topics? Do you feel competent in each of these areas? Or perhaps

People do not
live by
BREAD
ALONE,
but by every word
that comes from the
MOUTH
OF GOD.

MATTHEW 4:4

the opposite is the case. In the middle of reading, maybe you exclaim with the apostle Paul, "Who is sufficient for these things?" (2 Corinthians 2:16 RSV). It is my prayer that when that happens, you can say with confidence, "Christ is sufficient!"

Do you see? You have the one who obeyed all the commandments of the Father living His life in you. His life in you is what grants you His ability to have emotions that glorify Him, hold friendships that honor Him, stay away from impurity, embrace His design for sexuality, and live in community.

Knowing Christ—who is the truth—is all that is needed to abide firmly in Him until the end: "By his divine power, God has given us everything we need for living a godly life. We have received all of this by coming to know him, the one who called us to himself by means of his marvelous glory and excellence" (2 Peter 1:3).

Christ is the author and perfecter of our faith (Hebrews 12:2). Keep your eyes on Him until the day you finish your race here on this earth and forever enter into the joy of your Lord.

Remember what I believed was necessary to stand firm? It wasn't age or experience. That was assuming I had everything I needed. What I needed was another living in me and through me. I needed to read the Bible not as a step to accomplish something but as the only way that I could live. No YouTube tutorial compares with the sufficiency of Christ at our sides.

Now, more than longing for maturity, age, and experience, I want more of Jesus. "When I grow up," the only thing I want is the childlike dependence that Christ had. No matter how much He grew, He never abandoned His total trust in His Father.

Sometimes growing up is nothing more than admitting that we can't manage on our own, and giving glory to the One that can. And that is precisely where we discover our true strength.

Make It Personal

- Do you feel equipped to face the future? Why or why not? What difficulties or challenges has God allowed in your life to teach you that you alone cannot overcome the demands that lie before you?
- Praise God for Jesus Christ, for granting us complete rescue in Christ.
- When you face seemingly impossible demands, ask God to help you turn from your despair, anxiety, or anger and to Christ, to

discover more and more of who He is and how limitless His power is.

- Read Psalm 119 and ask God to use it to awaken an intense hunger for His Word in you.

FIVE

God Is My Designer

BETSY GÓMEZ

My oldest son is really into LEGO, and when he saw the Taj Mahal set, he was stunned. It had been in storage in our friends' garage for about ten years. Seeing Josué's reaction, our friends told him, "If you want it, we'll give it to you. Take it, break it all apart, and then build it again." He was speechless and couldn't believe it. How was he going to put together an almost six-thousand-piece project? But then they offered him the four instruction booklets they had held on to in case they needed to make repairs.

With his mouth still hanging open, Josué accepted the gift. At only ten years of age, he accepted the challenge. With a lot of dedication and persistence, he took the palace apart, washed the pieces, and sorted them into individual bags. He then spent the whole summer following the instructions step-by-step. When he finished, we did not see the Colosseum or the Great Wall of China. We saw the creation that the instruction manual had on its cover: the Taj Mahal.

Anyone can recognize that the correct way to assemble thousands of marble-colored pieces is by following the designer's instructions to the letter. The LEGO creators had determined how each piece should fit together. That type of project doesn't allow for redesigns or modifications. Success consists of reflecting the image of the original design.

It's easy to follow instructions when we're dealing with a LEGO set. But when it comes to our lives, we resist receiving orders. There is something in us that makes us reluctant to let others define what we are or what we should do. Have you ever—even deep down—resisted someone telling you how to live? I have.

This statement from actress Uzo Aduba summarizes the mindset of this generation: "I love this idea from neo-feminism: define yourself as you want, how you want to be today, and you can change tomorrow, and you can change the day after."

The voices of this world shout at us, "Follow your instincts! Obey your heart! Do whatever you want with your life, as many times as you want!" And if we're honest, it sounds like an attractive plan, but there is a truth that bursts our bubble. *We were created.*

COPYRIGHTS

If we had created ourselves, we'd have the copyright to do whatever seems best with our lives. But that is not the case. We were created by God. Our designer defined our worth, functions, and purpose. He didn't ask whether we were in agreement with His plan, nor did He provide an alternative design for His work. Do you know why? Because everything that God has made is very good (read Genesis 1:1–28).

> In the beginning God created the heavens and the earth. . . .
>
> And God saw that *it was* good.
>
> Then God said, "*Let us make human beings in our image, to be like us.* They will reign over the fish in the sea, the birds in the sky, the livestock, all the wild animals on the earth, and the small animals that scurry along the ground."
>
> So *God created human beings in his own image.*
> *In the image of God he created them;*
> *male and female he created them.*
> (Genesis 1:1, 25–28)

Everything that God has made is very good.

God—in His sovereignty—took the initiative to create all things, and He called them into existence through the power of His Word. He declared that His creation was good. Everything worked perfectly.

Later He created man and woman in His image, to be like Him. He formed man from the dust of the ground and breathed life into him (2:7). Look at how the story zooms in on the moment He creates the woman. (Open your Bible or Bible app and read Genesis 2:18–25.)

> Then the LORD God said, "It is not good for the man to be alone. *I will make a helper who is just right for him.*" . . .
> *. . . Then the LORD God made a woman from the rib, and he brought her to the man.*
> "At last!" the man exclaimed.
>
> "This one is bone from my bone,
> and flesh from my flesh!
> She will be called 'woman,'
> because she was taken from 'man.'"
> (verses 2:18, 22–23)

We have a saying in my country, "Clear as a rooster's crow." It's like saying, "It doesn't get any clearer than that." God is our Creator. Therefore, He has supreme authority over our lives. When he finished creating man and woman, do you know what He said? That His work was "very good" (1:31). Look at what the verses that you just read say:

The woman—just like the man—is made in God's image.

That is very good.

God gave the woman a different role than the man and assigned both the same purpose: to manifest His glory.

That is very good.

God formed the man first, then made the woman from his rib and brought her to the man.

That is very good.

God created the woman to be the ideal helper and so reflect His character as the helper of His people.

That is very good.

God gave the woman—unlike the man—a more fragile and delicate body with the strong ability to produce and nurture life.

That is very good.

So, if the God of all goodness, perfection, justice, sovereignty, holiness, power, and glory declares that all this is so extremely good, what should our responses be? The logical response would be to accept it with joy!

But sadly, that is not the response the world gives to God's design for women. Sadder still, it's not even the response of many women, young and not so young, who claim to be believers. I was one of them.

While in church, I bought into the world's ideas about what it means to be a woman, and I ignored what God said. I was a human and "Christian" version of the Powerpuff Girls. Have you ever seen that show?

I always thought that I could express my femininity however I wanted, and as long as I wrapped it all up with the phrase "for the glory of God," everything would be fine.

I thought that men and women were called by God to do the exact same things in the home and in the church. I fought to prove that there was nothing a man could do that I couldn't do better. Because of that, I didn't value motherhood, and deep down, I saw it as an obstacle to my success. I didn't want anyone to label me with the role of housewife because that made me feel useless. Whenever I heard words along the lines of "an ideal helper," it triggered a bomb inside me because I understood it as a synonym for "being a person of lower status."

That was twenty-five-year-old Betsy, who had a career in marketing and a master's degree in communication. I always escaped to my job as an excuse for my lack of responsibility around the house and my detachment from my newborn baby. My motto was "If somebody else can take care of the ordinary things, I can take care of the extraordinary ones." I didn't want to be a servant; I preferred to go out into the workplace to exercise my leadership skills and seek approval.

That is, until I ran across our Designer's instructions. One night when I wasn't able to sleep, I remembered that my husband had mentioned something about a conference called True Woman. I googled it and found a talk by Nancy DeMoss Wolgemuth titled "What Is a True Woman?" It seemed interesting, and I decided to watch it because I was looking for a little encouragement, and my inner voice was telling me, "That's exactly what I am, a true woman."

Ha, ha, ha!

It didn't take long for me to realize that this talk wasn't exactly what I had in mind. The Word of God showed me that my way of living was contrary to the faith that I professed. For the first time, I could see the sin that made me despise God's design for me. It all boiled down to my wanting to be my own authority.

That night I stayed awake till sunrise. God granted me repentance and forgiveness and helped me connect the dots between the gospel and my womanhood.

The Danger of Not Following the Instructions

It was eye-opening to realize how sin had affected my ability to see what God had made as a good thing. That didn't start with me; it was like this from the beginning. Let's look at how things went in Eden.

In the beginning, God gave clear instructions. He provided everything that a human being would need but also gave a restriction and said that the result of disobedience would be death:

> The Lord God warned him, "You may freely eat the fruit of every tree in the garden—except the tree of the knowledge of good and evil. If you eat its fruit, you are sure to die." (Genesis 2:16–17)

However, Satan entered the scene, and his target was the woman. He subtly planted doubt in her heart about the truthfulness of the command that God had given them.

> *Did God really say* you must not eat the fruit from any of the trees in the garden? (3:1)

The Enemy of God twisted what God had said, making Him seem like a tyrant. God had given them the freedom to eat from any tree in the garden, except one.

> Did God really say you must not eat the fruit from *any* of the trees in the garden? (verse 1)

He made her believe that if she disobeyed, she wouldn't suffer the consequences. Through this, he presented God as a liar.

> "*You won't die!*" the serpent replied to the woman. (verse 4)

And he attacked her heart directly by promising that her disobedience would elevate her to the throne of her life. He lied to her, saying that she could be her own god.

> God knows that your eyes will be opened as soon as you eat it, and *you will be like God,* knowing both good and evil. (verse 5)

She believed the great lie. Eve thought that she could become her own authority and set the rules of the game of her life.

> The woman was convinced. She saw that the tree was beautiful and its fruit looked delicious, and she wanted

> the wisdom it would give her. So she took some of the fruit and ate it. Then she gave some to her husband, who was with her, and he ate it, too. (verse 6)

From that moment on, nothing was the same.

Do you see? It all started because a woman didn't follow the instructions. Because a woman wanted to be her own authority. Sin has affected every human being born since then. We continue doubting the goodness of God. We choose to disobey, thinking that we will suffer no consequences and that we can be the supreme authority over our lives.

Sin has blinded our eyes so that we cannot see God's goodness and the beauty of His divine design.

When we take a look at our generation—and at our hearts—we recognize that something is wrong. It's clear that we haven't followed the instructions. Things were not meant to be this way. What do we see? Women trying to redefine themselves. Women who

- redefine their sexuality according to how they feel;
- decide whether their children live or die in the womb;
- redefine marriage, choosing to unite with other women;
- redefine their roles in the home because they don't want to feel like slaves;
- redefine success as making themselves the center of their lives;
- redefine the use of their bodies;
- are confused;
- have eaten the fruit of "do whatever you want"; and
- who need to know the truth.

Sin has blinded our eyes so that we cannot see God's goodness and the beauty of His divine design.

If you look at Romans 1:18–32, you'll see how we got to this point. Humans insist on rejecting the truth of God. They do not recognize His authority, and they deny His goodness. Instead of responding with gratitude for what God has done, they rebel against His design, and what is the result? Darkened hearts and confused minds.

Because of this rebellion and ingratitude, God has given them up to the worst of consequences: He let them do what they wanted. There is nothing more foolish than going against God in all His wisdom!

Do you see? Every attempt to redefine what God has already called good is an act of rebellion and ingratitude against God. It's a statement that screams, "You were wrong, God! I can do better than You! You are not enough to satisfy me. I have to create new ways to get what you cannot give me."

Every attempt to redefine what God has already called good is an act of rebellion and ingratitude against God.

Ultimately, redefining is about our misguided search for satisfaction.

That is the essence of all sin: seeking satisfaction in something other than God. We think we'll find freedom if only we can free ourselves from God. We search for what only God can give us in people, in relationships, in sex, in the use of our bodies . . . We think that power or control will give us happiness. We redefine the rules of the game because we see it as the solution to our problem.

Someone Followed the Instructions in Our Place!

So, amid so much confusion, what can we do? How can this mess be fixed?

The only solution for sin can be found in the person of Jesus Christ. He already followed God's instructions perfectly, and He did it for us. The only way to return to God's design is to believe the good news of the gospel.

No matter how messed up our lives may seem, we have hope because the gospel restores all things!

The gospel is the power of God to put to death all rebellion that rises against the truth. It is the power of God to change our affections and transform our priorities. The gospel frees us from the idea that we can be our own authorities, and prepares us to fulfill the purpose we were created for.

The lens of the gospel helps us see the goodness of God in Christ and find the satisfaction that we long for in Him. We can respond to God with gratitude and clearly see the beauty of His design.

The gospel changes my rebellious cry for independence to a declaration of absolute and joyful surrender to the authority of God. It enables me to declare these truths:

- "God is my supreme authority."
- "I am a creation of God."
- "I'm a disciple of Christ."
- "I am a daughter of God."
- "I am a life-giver."
- "I'm a suitable helper."
- "My design as a woman is beautiful!"
- "I express my womanhood as a response to the gospel."
- "My womanhood serves to reflect aspects of God's character that a man cannot show by himself."
- "I am a woman for the glory of God!"

You, too, can put on the lens of the gospel and appreciate the beauty of your design. My prayer is that you become a young woman rooted in the truth. One who believes and practices the following things in her daily life:

- A young woman who recognizes God as her designer surrenders to His will instead of trying to redefine herself according to the world's standards.
- A young woman surrendered to the lordship of Christ governs her identity—sexuality, relationships, and lifestyle—by the truth of God's Word, not by her feelings or the pressure of the world.
- A young woman renewed by the Holy Spirit exhibits the heart of a biblical woman through the fruit of the Spirit: love, joy, peace, patience, kindness, goodness, faithfulness, gentleness, and self-control.
- A young woman who has embraced the truth of the gospel recognizes that biblical womanhood is not just a step in her faith walk but the result of walking as a disciple of Christ.
- A young woman who accepts her womanhood with joy has no need to fight for validation or respect. She knows her Creator and what He has said of her.
- A young woman who takes up her cross every day and follows Christ is not afraid to display her Lord's character in her way of living.
- A young woman who is seated in heavenly places in Christ does not need to strive for the top spots.
- A young woman who is complete in Christ does not seek the approval of people.

- A young woman who has been born again to a living hope joyfully embraces her role as a life-giver to those around her.
- A young woman who has been marked by the meekness and humility of Christ reflects a tender, serene spirit, regardless of her personality.
- A young woman transformed by the gospel is not afraid of biblical submission because she knows that she is ultimately submitting to her Lord and Savior.
- A young woman who has experienced the forgiveness of her sins by the redemptive work of Christ on the cross extends forgiveness to those who have offended her.
- A young woman who has experienced the saving help of her God is not ashamed to be a suitable helper in her context.
- A young woman who has her identity in Christ is not consumed by the desire to prove something to the world.
- A young woman who longs to please God in all things knows that she can't do so in her own strength. She depends on God in every aspect of her life.
- A young woman who stands firm in the truth clothes herself with the gospel, the armor of God.
- A young woman who is hidden in God embraces the calling that He has for her life without fear of the future.

Draw Near to Your Good God

Jackie Hill Perry was a young lesbian woman who rejected the traditional image of what it means to be a woman. In His grace, God saved her and opened her eyes to the beauty of His design. The transformation the gospel has produced in her is amazing. In an interview with Revive Our Hearts, she said, "When I saw that God created me to be a woman, and that being a woman is a good thing, that's when I started to embody femininity . . . because my theology preceded my affections. But when [I understood this], my affections and my theology reconciled and became one."[1]

Considering God's goodness and believing that all He has done is good is a vital step if we want to embrace His design and will for our lives. We need to see Him. We need to run to Christ and let His Word define who we are.

I love how Jackie invites us to silence the voices of this world and pay attention to what God—our good God—says about us. Here is one of her poems, "What Is a Woman?"[2]

The other day a young lady, brown as the melanin in my daughter's eyes
Said behind a mic that she hated being a woman.
She wanted to know what it meant to be one.
And I have often wondered the same.

I looked around for the teaching of such to tell me of myself.
We all learn to be by imitation or indoctrination.
Mama and media can't help but train,
Tutor us into carbon copies of themselves
So then, knowing who we are or what we should be,
Is really understanding whose costumes we wear on most days,

Whose skeletons we switched with when Adam took his nap.

I was told a woman could not truly be herself.
That is, if herself is not light enough, dark enough, or if her hair is the Rapunzel replica,
Or if it to be Underground Railroad, for those cotton active men to stomach.

I was told that my body is neither belonging to me nor its beauty innate,
But that I am not gorgeous unless told by another woman's son to be so.
When did the mouth of men, in whose image women are not made in,
Begin to damage us so silently?
Maybe it was when we began believing the voices that have no deity in it.

I was told a woman should not submit, should not be meek,
That that type of behavior was only for women who treated their voice like a secret.

I was told not to be a secret but a siren, to be as Moschetti as I can

And honor my opinions at the expense of respect.

While some men may believe themselves to have liberty
over a woman's body
And taught how to destroy as only depravity can
predict.
We have equally learned how to tear and rip
And undo dignity with a mere sentence or a squint.
It's called strong by society.
They tell us that's what a backbone looks like.

But beautiful is the spine that remembers where it came
from,
The Lexus knowing of self.
Not being determined by every wind of doctrine and dust,
but God Himself.
We must alert the deep misunderstandings that compose
themselves
As empowerment, as freedom.

Liberation has never come by way of unbelief.
Eve another taillight by finding beauty in lies,
But only a naked body and a husband that forgot her first
name.

We women must be smarter, must be wiser,
Must be bent on loving truth no matter how contradicting
it is to a dying culture.

I tell you: A woman is no fool unless she chooses to be.
If you ask me, "What is a woman?"
I would tell you that she is a bone made alive with distinc-
tions that set her apart,
As does the difference between a firefly and a new poem.

A woman is not a man.
Her calling is not a synonym of inferiority.
Her distinctions are not the child of patriarchy.

They come from a creative God.
Did you see His fingerprints in your hips?

The whistling shadow of His mind when your body became home to another name
That called you Mommy while all the gladness you forgot could exist.

A woman submits to her God, her husband, her church.
She is no weak-willed or brittle-backed woman,
But only as strong as humility and faith may identify her to be.

They say, "Submission sounds like servant."
They say, "That sounds like something to rebel against."

I say, "Ain't it funny that servant is repulsive to everyone but God?"
And we wonder why we can't recognize His face.

If you asked me, "What is a woman?"
I would tell you that she is a sister to all,
Even those whose blood is not of the same roots,
But who is still as kin as her mama's firstborn.

And she treats these sisters like a wintered quilt,
Making sure her mouth does not unstitch that which was made to keep cold hearts warm.

We are made up of nurture and everything comfortable,
And that is why we feel so deep, why we cry so sudden.
Because the emotions that make us woman,
Don't make us unstable but earnest refuse to the chaos where our ribs once set
We are necessary and nuanced at best.

But a woman should be nothing more or less than what God made her to be.
Anything that defines our being,
That does not shimmer and sing of Christ and His wisdom,
Is a definition destined for flames.

If you asked me, "What is a woman?"
I would simply tell you, "Ask God who made her."

Draw near to your Creator and behold His goodness in Jesus. I assure you that you will see—in full color—the goodness of His character and the beauty of the design that sin has tried to obscure. You will cultivate a heart willing to be shaped according to the instructions of the Designer. And you will do so with joy because in Christ, you will find the freedom, fullness, and abundance that you long for.

Make It Personal

- Have you ever resisted someone telling you what to do or say?
- You are God's creation. How does the truth change your perspective of how you should live?
- Is there an area of your life that you need to surrender to the authority of God?
- How does the gospel free you to surrender to your Creator?

SIX

God Decides My Value

BETHANY BEAL

I looked at myself in the mirror and knew exactly what I was missing. More eyeliner. I'm not referring to delicate lines around my eyes to highlight them. No. I mean enough eyeliner to make me look like a raccoon. I mean loads and loads above and below my eyes. I mean so much eyeliner that anyone could literally mistake me for a raccoon.

Yes. That was my go-to look in high school.

I went out of my way to draw the boys' attentions. I craved feeling and looking beautiful. I wanted to be noticed with all my heart. I longed to be a desirable woman. I longed for the inner satisfaction I thought external beauty could bring me. My way of calling attention to myself and looking beautiful was putting on huge amounts of eyeliner.

Years later, in my early twenties, not much had changed. Yes, by that time I had stopped using eyeliner, but my inner longing to be beautiful in the eyes of others was still alive and well. I had the same empty heart, just a new strategy for filling it. Instead of putting on eyeliner, I was obsessed with having perfect skin. I couldn't accept any acne or skin blemishes. In the depths of my heart, I believed having smooth skin made me worth more. Deep down in my heart, I believed it would give me worth in the eyes of others. Especially men.

I'll never forget the day I saw myself in the mirror and noticed that I had several pimples around my mouth and on my chin. I leaned in closer to see them better and evaluate the damage. I remember feeling so upset at that outbreak. I immediately started to fear what my friends would think of me. What would boys think? I wondered whether they were going to think I wasn't as pretty because of the zits. I wondered whether they would care about me less. I even asked myself whether they would still want to be my friends. I allowed the Enemy's lie to enter my mind. I convinced myself that my worth depended entirely on my appearance and what other people thought of me.

Thankfully, God didn't allow those fears to keep dominating my mind. God allowed me to lay my insecurities aside for a moment and reminded me that I was His daughter. He reminded me that nobody could add or take away from my worth as a person. I went back to look at myself in the mirror and thought, "If my friends stop caring about me because I have a zit on my skin, they're not real friends. What friend devalues a person for something as superficial as a pimple?" That moment in front of the mirror was one of my first steps toward lasting freedom. God gave me the confidence to meet up with my friends and enjoy the night without fearing what they thought of me. I surrendered my appearance to God and did my best to trust in He who loved me with or without pimples.

God reminded me that nobody could add or take away from my worth as a person.

I started to read the Word of God more intentionally. I started to listen more attentively to the wisdom of my parents and mentors. Slowly but surely, I started to better understand and believe that my value had nothing to do with the approval of guys, friends, or companions, and conversely had everything to do with the value that God had already assigned me as His daughter.

In retrospect, those years of striving for the "perfect look" fill me with both sadness and joy. Sadness for having wasted so much energy looking for lasting worth in empty solutions. And joy because I've moved so far beyond that and have discovered powerful truths that transformed my life, my perspective on beauty, and my value as a woman. I know the topic of beauty is a struggle for many young people, if not the majority. It seems like achieving the "perfect look" has been a serious obsession for women throughout history and in all cultures. But, as many of us have learned through personal experience, this effort to achieve fulfillment and satisfaction through a perfect look has not given us the results we've hoped for.

Throughout this chapter, I want to share the four powerful truths that have completely transformed my life. They have infused me with confidence, security, and the courage to live each day for the glory of God (despite how I look and feel in certain moments). If you've struggled with the idea of beauty at some point, my prayer is that these four biblical truths change your life and offer you the freedom and fulfillment that your heart longs for.

Four Powerful Truths to Embrace True Beauty and Lasting Worth

1. God Is the Inventor of Beauty

I love remembering the beginning of creation. The Bible tells us that the earth was formless and void. There was nothing on it. There were no flowers or clouds or fluffy bunnies or dawns or sunsets. There was nothing but empty space. That description doesn't seem very beautiful to me. Does it to you?

The reason I like to start with those formless and empty moments is because, soon after, God did something monumental. He, displaying His power and creativity, decided to take what was nothing and turn it into something magnificent. Let's take a peek at what God did on the first day of creation. (I know that we've already talked about Genesis in previous chapters, but believe me, it's worth it!) You can look up the complete passage in Genesis 1 and 2.

> In the beginning God created the heavens and the earth. The earth was formless and empty, and darkness covered the deep waters. And the Spirit of God was hovering over the surface of the waters.
>
> Then God said, "Let there be light," and there was light. And God saw that the light was good. Then He separated the light from the darkness. God called the light "day" and the darkness "night."
>
> And evening passed and morning came, marking the first day. (1:1–5).

God continued His work and created the heavens, oceans, mountains, plants, trees, vegetation, sun and moon, water-dwelling creatures, and beasts of the earth. After He had finished all of that, God made His ultimate creation. First the man and then the woman. All was absolutely perfect and formed by God Himself.

Take a moment to think with me about what we've just read. God was able to create anything. He could have made the world simple, boring, and uninteresting. But He didn't. He created everything with great care and precision. He made it absolutely beautiful. It was spectacular. Think of the beauty of even the sunset. To contemplate it sometimes leaves us in awe. It was God who gave us all that. He made the sun rise in the morning and set in the evening, and He gave us the ability to appreciate and enjoy it.

What does this talk about creation have to do with beauty? It has everything to do with beauty. If we don't understand where beauty comes from, we'll never be able to embrace it biblically. God created us, as Christian women, with the ability to appreciate beauty. We watch a sunset, and it leaves us awestruck and dazzled. We didn't create this ability—God gave it to us. In the same way, He created us to be beautiful women. He deliberately designed us. Each curve, each shape, and each aspect of our womanhood was designed by our loving Creator. He gave us women a special kind of beauty. It's good to appreciate and enjoy our femininity.

I encourage you to think about femininity like a beautiful bouquet of flowers. What gives them their splendor? Variety. The combination of flowers. The different fragrances. The colors. The textures. The lengths. Variety is what makes a bouquet so special. The same goes for young women. God created a beautiful variety for us to appreciate. Some are tall, others short. Some are light-skinned, others are dark-skinned. Some have thick lips, and others very thin ones. Some have thick hair, others thin. Some have light-colored eyes, others dark. Each detail of God's design of womanhood is what makes women so beautiful. Let's choose to embrace the unique beauty God has given us in the same way we accept a beautiful bouquet.

2. *God Designed Me, so He Defines My Worth*

A few years ago, I went to breakfast with my dad. We parked by the diner, walked through the front doors, and were met by a hostess who stared at me, open-mouthed. Without greeting or welcoming us, she stared at me in utter shock. She looked me up and down, then said, "You are freakishly tall." I stood there perplexed. I didn't know what to say. This woman just called me a freak because I was tall. Let's just say it was a very awkward and uncomfortable moment. It's true that I'm tall, just over six feet. But I'd never considered myself a freak. This was the first time someone said something like that to me.

I had a choice to make. I could get angry and mourn over the fact that I was so tall. I could believe the lie that I was less valuable or less worthy because someone considered me freakishly tall. I could sink into depression and never leave my house again for fear that someone would call me something worse. I had to make a choice, and I had to do it quickly!

Thankfully, I had the Word of God stored in my heart to help me confront that rude comment about my height. Instead of slipping into depression or resenting the fact that I was (and am) so tall, I simply remembered that I was a child of God. He had made me in my mother's womb. I decided to praise Him because I was amazingly and wonderfully made. If He hadn't wanted me to be six feet, one inch tall, I wouldn't be so. But that's how He wanted me. He formed me perfectly to be the tall woman that I am today.

> You [God] made all the delicate, inner parts of my body
> and knit me together in my mother's womb.
> Thank you for making me so wonderfully complex!
> Your workmanship is marvelous—how well I know it.
> You watched me as I was being formed in utter seclusion,
> as I was woven together in the dark of the womb.
> (Psalm 139:13–15)

This passage makes it clear to us: God is the only one who has the authority to define what makes us valuable. We should remember that He is our Creator and Maker. Nobody else (including guys, culture, Hollywood, friends, social media) has the right to say what we are worth. They did not create us; they have no authority. In truth, their opinion doesn't matter. Only our Creator has the authority to determine what gives us value and worth.

God is the only one who has the authority to define what makes us valuable.

Psalm 139 is what helped me fight the lie that I was a freak. I'm sure this passage can help you too. Instead of believing you have to look like the "ideal" woman, stop and remember that you are God's perfect creation. He doesn't make mistakes. He formed you and says that His works are marvelous. Instead of complaining about your height, the shape of your nose, the color of your skin, the texture of your hair, or any other aspect of your appearance, take some time to praise God for forming you perfectly and designing you exactly as He wanted. Marvelous are His works. That includes you.

3. God Is Interested in My Heart

In a world that literally worships a woman's physical appearance, it can be difficult to avoid being trapped in that mentality. When we pass by a magazine in the store and see a beautiful woman on the cover with words that say

"Long live the queen" or "The sexiest woman in the world," it can be tempting to measure our value and worth based on physical appearance. Beauty is a reality that God designed, but not as the principal characteristic of our womanhood.

Again and again in the Scriptures, we find that God used the humble, the weak, the outcast, and the marginalized to carry out His plans. God is not measuring us by our physical appearances. He isn't picking favorites according to what the world publishes on its magazine covers. Indeed, He often does the exact opposite. He uses what the world considers "less than" to do extraordinary work for His kingdom. He delights in using those who are humble at heart. "God opposes the proud but gives grace to the humble" (James 4:6).

Beauty is a reality that God designed, but not as the principal characteristic of our womanhood.

Instead of spending so much time worrying about our external appearances and trying to make them perfect, we should concentrate more on the conditions of our hearts. Can you imagine how different our lives would be if we dedicated more time to our hearts and being more like Christ? We would be free of the weight and the burden of living in comparison to others. We would finally be free to praise God and serve Him to the fullest with the bodies He has given us. We wouldn't live enslaved to the images we see on social media, other people's comments, or the slightest attention a guy provides us. Nothing is that important. The only thing of importance would be the opinion of our Savior and Creator.

There's a passage in the Old Testament that clearly shows the heart God has for people. To Him, it doesn't matter how attractive or strong a person is. What truly matters is the condition of their heart.

> The Lord said to Samuel, "Don't judge by his appearance or height, for I have rejected him. The Lord doesn't see things the way you see them. People judge by outward appearance, but the Lord looks at the heart." (1 Samuel 16:7)

What a crucial reminder for each of us. We should change our mentality and truly evaluate who and what we choose to praise. Are we trapped in worshipping who the world considers worthy in light of their outward appearances? If so, we should take a step back and ask God to change our

Thank you for making me so wonderfully complex! Your workmanship is marvelous—how well I know it.

PSALM 139:14

hearts so that they're in tune with His. We also have to look inwardly and ask ourselves how we're measuring our own value. Is it the yardstick of the world or of God? Sometimes we can be too hard on ourselves because of the unreachable standard we've taken from our culture. We need to stop that. We have to see ourselves through the lens God sees us through. Humankind judges by outward appearance, but God looks at the heart. Let's choose to do the same.

4. God Created Me to Glorify and Serve Him with the Body He Gave Me

Earlier in life, I was the only one who mattered. My time, my money, my talents, my agenda, my friends, and my future were the only things that mattered. High school Bethany was very different from the Bethany I am today. Like many of you, a large part of my life was about myself. While I was a Christian and attended church regularly, I had fallen into the trap of self-centeredness. The world revolved around Bethany. It took many years and numerous trials to start understanding that I was created by someone greater than me. That someone was God.

This fourth and final truth is the most important one we'll cover. Until we understand that we were created to worship, praise, serve, and live for God completely, we'll indefinitely keep revolving, trying to live for the glory of our own names. Life is much bigger than us. Much, much bigger. The real reason God created us and gave us a body is so that we could have personal relationships with Him and serve Him with our lives.

> We are his workmanship, created in Christ Jesus for good works, which God prepared beforehand, that we should walk in them. (Ephesians 2:10 RSV)

If you believe it, this verse can change your life. You are His creation. He has good works for you to do. He has prepared them beforehand for you so that you can walk in them. God has awesome purposes for His daughters (for you and for me). He has the best intentions for our lives. He is interested in the details of our day-to-day lives, like what we do and why we do it. He hasn't given us bodies and external beauty so we can obsess over them or live for them. No. He has given us these things so we may serve Him better and walk in the good works that He has assigned to us. That is the ultimate reason He made our bodies. To glorify God.

Life is not ultimately about us. Our bodies are not about us. Our beauty and our femininity are not about us. Each one of us is God's handiwork, created for Christ Jesus. We were made to walk in the good works that Christ has prepared for us.

We must shift from being self-focused to being Christ-focused. When we stop gazing at ourselves and focus on living for Christ, something radical happens to our perspective. It stops being an insecure, self-centered viewpoint and becomes a confident, Christ-centered one. That shift leads to a life full of confidence because it's about living for a purpose greater than attracting people's attention or winning others' approval.

We must shift from being self-focused to being Christ-focused.

Looking back on the different steps of my life during adolescence, single life, relationships and breakups, marriage, and now pregnancy, I can't avoid asking myself where I would be if I hadn't learned the truth. I know that I would probably not be writing this chapter and opening up my heart to you. My hope and prayer is that you take this truth and ask God to change your heart and help you live a life dedicated to Him. Only then will you find the freedom that your heart truly longs for.

Focus on Embracing the Four Powerful Truths

When I remember my high school years and those days of raccoon-ish eyeliner, I wish I'd understood and embraced these four powerful truths sooner. They have transformed me into a satisfied, grateful woman focused on Christ. I'm a much more confident woman because I understand where my value as a woman comes from. Let's choose to be girls who embrace God's liberating design for true, long-lasting beauty.

Make It Personal

- Which of the four powerful truths do you need to embrace the most, and why?
- Have you looked in the mirror and disliked something about yourself? How did you handle that moment?

- Why is it so important to understand that God formed you in your mother's womb? Look up Psalm 139:13–15 for a reminder.
- Read 1 Samuel 16:7. How should God's perspective on physical strength and outward beauty change the way you see yourself and others?
- How can you better serve God with the body He gave you?

SEVEN

God Has Given Me Emotions for His Glory

AYLÍN MICHELÉN DE MERCK

We were about to board the plane. A feeling of panic, one that I wasn't unfamiliar with, started to grow inside me. I breathed and tried to ignore what fear was telling me. I'm claustrophobic, and while flying itself doesn't scare me, being inside a plane can make me feel trapped.

As I was walking to our seats, *Fear* began sounding the alarm. "You see?" it said to me. "You're in the last row. Exactly what you hate. And on top of that, there are no windows." I sat down on the row assigned to me with my little one in my arms. My heart was starting to race a bit. *Fear* continued: "You think you'll last two hours here? You're going to have a panic attack."

How was I going to respond to what *Fear* was telling me?

EMOTIONS ARE A GIFT

Sometimes I wish I could get rid of the emotions I feel so intensely and are sometimes so hard to control. But there is a reality I have to keep in mind: Emotions are a gift from God. They tell us many things that are true and allow us to experience life more fully. I thank God for giving me the gift of experiencing the deep love of my husband, the exquisite tenderness of holding my babies in my arms, and the delight I feel when enjoying the ocean in front of me. Can you imagine what life would be like if everything were always the same? If you couldn't taste chocolate ice cream with chocolate sauce? Or if you couldn't enjoy riding a roller coaster?

Emotions are also a gift because, through them, we show the world the emotions of God. He loves His children with a deep love (Isaiah 43:4). His heart is full of compassion for those who fear Him (Psalm 103:13). He rejoices in His people so much that he even sings with joy (Zephaniah 3:17). God experiences anger for sin and hates injustice (Proverbs 11:1). Our Father is jealous, and in His love, He keeps us only for Himself (Exodus 34:14).

However, because of our sin, sometimes emotions can also tell us things that aren't true. They shout loudly at us to get our attention. They want us to feel their urgency and act according to them.

When our emotions reflect the beautiful and holy character of God, our souls remain firm. But when emotions take control and serve another god, we stagger and lose our balance. In those moments, it's hard to think logically, we might act irrationally, and loving others becomes impossible.

When our emotions control us, they determine the "truth" according to which we live. It's as if we suddenly put on blue-tinted glasses and see everything in that color. The emotions become our master, and instead of obeying God and acting according to His truth, they make us worship other things instead of worshipping the one and only God, our Savior.

What can we do to make sure our emotions serve our Father and glorify Him?

We need to abide in Jesus Christ. When you feel emotions that do not reflect the holiness of God and that want to control you—whether it's depression, anxiety, fear, envy, anger, sadness, distrust, feelings of condemnation, or guilt—believe in Him. Believe that He conquered all those emotions, so He is your King, not them.

Don't put your faith in what you're able to feel, think, or do. Instead, put your faith in all that Christ is and all that He does in you and for you, even now:

- He has made you new.
- His gospel is the "power of God for salvation" (Romans 1:16 RSV), not just when you're first converted—it's also the power that you need to live right now.
- Jesus lives in you (Galatians 2:20).
- Jesus conquered all unholy emotions. He has the last word (not them).
- Jesus is continually transforming you and will finish the work that He started (Philippians 1:6).
- Jesus is praying for you (Hebrews 7:25).
- Jesus has the power to save all who are tested (Hebrews 2:18).

If we believe He laid down His life for us and calls us friends (John 15:13–15), we must now show that we are His friends by doing what He asks of us.

As we mentioned in chapter 4, believing in Christ is shown through a life that depends on God through the Word and prayer. When we abide in Jesus, we live like Peter when he said, "To whom would we go? You have the words that give eternal life" (John 6:68). In this chapter, you will see again and again the importance of the Word of God. The Word is the truth of God (17:17) and defines true reality. When we abide in His Word, we find the healing our souls urgently long for.

TRAIN-ING

Imagine a train with three parts: the engine, the main car, and the last car. The engine defines the reality of the train. The main car follows, and the caboose goes wherever the engine leads it.

The Word of God and His truth must be the engine of our lives. God's Word defines what is true and what our true reality is. We follow God's truth while our emotions follow like the last car, submitting to what the Bible commands. Sometimes emotions want to be the engine of our train and define our reality. But the good news is that if we are in Christ, we can train our emotions to submit to God's truth, stay in their place as the last car, and go wherever the Word leads!

If we are in Christ, we can train our emotions to submit to God's truth.

God plays a similar role in transforming the rest of our hearts. We can't train our hearts by ourselves. Instead, if we respond in faith to God's truth, He works the change we need.

When my emotions act as the engine and try to pull the main car another direction, I imagine them as bullies trying to intimidate me into believing them instead of my Father. Thank God we have Christ, who faces our bullies and defends us (Psalm 3).

For those times when you see that one of those bullies wants to control or intimidate you, I want to give you four strategies to train your emotions in the truth and use to put them back in the last car.

1. Speak the Truth About Your Father to Your Emotions

Notice that I didn't say to tell them just the truth about God. It's important that, when speaking to your emotions, you remind them of the kind of relationship you have with the God that made the heavens and the earth. Words fail me when I try to write what it means for us to know God as our Father. When we forget the loving relationship He has with us, the truth about God is no longer personal or close.

God is not just an impersonal, sovereign being who runs the universe. He is not even just a kindhearted monarch who sits on His throne, showing mercy to His subjects. If we are in Christ, we have the eternal gift of sharing in His Father (John 20:17). When our emotions want to decide where the train goes, nothing is more important for a daughter of God than knowing her Father well.

Worshipping our Father quiets our souls, renews our joy, and fills us with true peace.

Our Father is an eternal source of goodness, delighting in doing us good. He has gifted us the inheritance of His Son and has blessed us in Him with all spiritual blessings (Ephesians 1).

Because Christ is in our lives, it's important to observe His relationship with the Father. I love listening to how Jesus speaks with the Father in the Gospels. You can sense His trust in His Father's plan (John 6:36–40), His rest in His love (15:10), and how He longs to be with Him again (17:13). That trust, rest, and longing are already ours in Christ.

It is urgent to remember this whenever emotions want to define our reality. We have the life and power of Christ to recognize when they contradict the character and relationship we have with our Father. Usually when our emotions—not the holy ones—take control of the train, they tell us lies about God and make us forget His fatherhood.

- When envy wants you to believe that God is withholding something good from you, answer it by saying, "The Lord will withhold no good thing from those who do what is right" (Psalm 84:11).
- When anger tells you that God is unjust and that you have to fight to defend yourself, remind it that your Father hates injustice and defends those in need (Psalm 89:14).
- If depression ever wants to invade your heart, look it in the eyes and face it with courage: "My Father watches over me to rescue my soul from death and keep me alive in times of famine" (see Psalm 33:18–20).
- When fear makes you doubt the love of God, tell it, "See, God has come to save me. I will trust in Him and not be afraid.

> The LORD GOD is my strength and my song; he has given me victory" (Isaiah 12:2).

Our Father is trustworthy. Even though things don't make sense and it seems like God is making a mistake, we have the gift of knowing that Christ's trust in His Father is ours too. He never doubted that His Father would resurrect Him. He was convinced that His will was always good. Glory to God that we can follow Jesus in saying, "I want your will to be done, not mine" (Luke 22:42).

When I was on the airplane, *Fear* wanted me to forget that my Father's eyes were on me, controlling each detail to show me who He is. It was a comfort when the Spirit reminded me that God is my Daddy and that in my weakness, Jesus is my strength (2 Corinthians 12:9).

2. *Speak the Truth About Your Emotions to Your Father*

When you stand firm in your Father's abundant love, when you know you are safe in Christ and nobody can snatch you from His hand, the door is open for you to present yourself to your Father with confidence and say exactly how you feel.

Many times shame makes us hide our emotions from our Father. We know we shouldn't feel envy, discontentment, or anger. Like Adam and Eve, we use fig leaves to cover ourselves while hiding from God.

But hiding ourselves does not glorify God. It actually reveals that we have an unbiblical fear of Him and that we don't fully understand His heart for us in Christ. Christ has opened the door so that we may come confidently before the throne of our gracious God to receive all the help we need from His hand (Hebrews 4:16).

The book of Psalms is full of the heartfelt language of the psalmists, who expressed how they felt to God. Look, for example, at Psalm 13:

> O LORD, how long will you forget me? Forever?
> How long will you look the other way?
> How long must I struggle with anguish in my soul,
> with sorrow in my heart every day?
> How long will my enemy have the upper hand?
> (verses 1–2)

The psalmist was not afraid to ask God these questions. "How much longer will you allow me to be like this?" He admitted that he felt God had forgotten him. It seemed like God had hidden Himself from the psalmist . . . and he told God how he felt.

Psalm 88 is another example of the psalmist telling God all his problems. He confessed that he was a man without strength, and that he was like those God had forgotten. He even confessed that he knew it was God Himself who put him in that situation (verses 6–8).

Psalm after psalm, the psalmists speak with God in very open and heartfelt manners. At times their theologies aren't even correct—like, can God forget us? But I believe God allowed these prayers in Scripture to give us language for approaching Him. They also encourage us when nothing makes sense and we are completely lost.

And what about Jesus? Do we see Him approaching the Father with that type of openness?

Look at Luke 22 with me. Jesus knew that He was at the point of drinking the cup of God's wrath. He experienced great affliction. He even sweated drops of blood because He could foresee the agony that awaited Him. And what did He do in that moment? Did He try to distract Himself with His friends? Ease His pain a little with comfort food? No, He turned to the Father. He poured out His heart before Him. He begged Him: "Father, if you are willing, please take this cup of suffering away from me" (verse 42). His Father didn't take the cup away, but He did send an angel to strengthen Him.

When Christ was on the cross, He cried, "My God, my God, why have you abandoned me?" quoting Psalm 22. He was not afraid to open His heart to His Father or ask Him why. Asking God questions is not a sin. While your heart is turned to God (and not moving away from Him), you will always find grace and help when you approach Him, even with questions, confusion, and pain.

You experience many different emotions every day. You open your eyes and think about what lies ahead (perhaps a test, difficult conversation, painful memory, or friend that is hard to love). You see yourself tempted to feel anxiety, sadness, anger, or rejection. And later you realize you've been dominated by that emotion. Don't try to suppress or hide it in shame!

In that moment, with the life and power of Christ in you, turn to your Father who loves you and tell Him what is in your heart. Confess if you have sinned. Tell Him about the weakness you feel and that you are unable to fight all your emotions. Christ lives to save those who approach Him by the way He opened to the Father through His blood (Hebrews 10:19; 7:25).

3. Speak the Truth About Yourself to Your Emotions

It's Monday morning. You've just opened your eyes. You're still in bed. You decide to scroll through Instagram to see if your best friend sent you a message. She hasn't sent you anything. But you keep at it, scrolling past picture after picture after picture.

SEE,

GOD HAS COME

TO **SAVE** ME.

I WILL

TRUST IN HIM

AND NOT BE

AFRAID.

ISAIAH 12:2

Your friend won an award in her choir. You tap the little heart to give it a like, but you feel real envy because you didn't win that award in the same class. Three photos later, you find a picture of your three friends from your neighborhood hanging out over the weekend, but they didn't invite you. Your heart sinks. "Why didn't they invite me? Did I do something wrong? Am I not cool enough?" You keep looking at photos, but now you're just trying to distract your feelings of sadness, shame, and real discouragement.

Finally, you find a photo of your cousin with a piece of artwork she drew. It's incredible; she's obviously really talented. On the one hand, you appreciate her work, but on the other, you ask yourself, What am I good for? What do I do well? You check the likes on her post. You compare them to the likes you received on your last photo, and she has a lot more. Suddenly you feel that everyone in the world is better than you. It brings you down.

I'm very familiar with that situation. It's happened to me a lot. Social media can be a great blessing. But it can also turn into a place of comparison and competition. When I'm not resting in Christ and His gospel, it's easy for me to fall into the temptation of believing that what others think of me is what defines me. I feel like I have to prove myself. I measure my value by the number of likes or interactions my posts have. I compare my life to others to see who is better and who seems like they have it all together.

In those moments, abiding in Christ is vital. Who defines you? Does your identity change daily based on what social media tells you? Or does it remain forever?

Remember that if you have placed your faith in Christ, you exist in Him, and He in you. Whether you have many likes or just a few, your identity is rooted in these truths:

- You live in Christ.
- Christ lives in you.
- You are a new creation.

Living in Christ means there is an invisible reality that defines you. When you are lying in bed feeling down, there's a greater truth that shapes every moment you live on this earth. If you died with Christ, you also rose with Him, and you are now seated with Him in the heavenly places (Ephesians 2:6). That means that you are seated in a place of victory and authority. Christ has given you His honor. In Christ, God loves you with a strong, constant love. Forever and ever, God will demonstrate the abundant riches of His grace in His goodness toward us in Christ Jesus.

Christ lives forever in you, and you in Him.

As we said in chapter 4, you already belong to Christ and are abiding in Him. Remember that abiding in Christ means believing in Him.

- Believe that all the emotions of Christ are yours. His steadfast love, pure and sacrificial, is yours; His joy, His zeal for His Father, His humility . . . He has given them to you.
- Believe that you are firmly and securely united with Christ. You are part of His vine. No emotional struggle can tear you away from that strong trunk binding you to Him.
- Believing that Christ lives in you can overcome emotions that sometimes feel stronger than you.

If your emotions are trying to make you feel that you are in a place of desperation or abandonment, if they want you to think that God has forgotten you because you are not sufficient . . . tell them the story of the fervent love the Father has for you in Christ Jesus.

Believing that Christ lives in you can overcome emotions that sometimes feel stronger than you.

4. Speak the Truth About Your Circumstances to Your Emotions

I have physical limitations that sometimes affect me emotionally. Certain foods can make me feel down and discouraged, while monthly hormonal changes can also sometimes bring feelings of anxiety and panic. Additionally, when I've not exercised for several weeks, my body struggles to manage the stress that comes from living in the Middle East, raising three children, and learning another language without much support. My body becomes overwhelmed more quickly, and I am particularly affected by the temptation to feel anxious for no apparent reason.

In those moments, my emotions try to define my reality. They tell me:

- "You're about to receive really bad news."
- "That tragedy you're so afraid of will happen."
- "You're right to feel guilty."
- "You hurt this or that person, and there'll surely be conflict with them over it."
- "That pain you're feeling is cancer."

Our emotions are responses to real circumstances. You feel anxious because you don't have a boyfriend. Or maybe a friend has betrayed you, and anger seems to have taken up permanent residence. Perhaps you've experienced a painful loss and now live in fear of facing another.

My friend, in those circumstances, run to the Father and run to His Word. Speak with Him but also listen to His voice through His Word. Let His Word speak to your emotions. The more you know the truth, the more God will use what you know about Him to train your heart.

Recently I've felt my weaknesses and limitations. The psalms have reoriented my heart. Here are a few that I'd like to share with you:

- The name of God is good and worthy of trust (Psalm 54:6).
- None who hope in the Lord will ever be disgraced (25:3).
- "All the paths of the LORD are steadfast love and faithfulness" (verse 10 RSV).
- We can trust everything he does (33:4).

I invite you to do what I've done. Read Psalms and let the Word—living and effective—diagnose your heart, renew your hope, and feed your joy.

The more you know the truth, the more God will use what you know about Him to train your heart.

God has created you with emotions. That part of His good plan was there from the very beginning. It's true that sin distorted His design. But Christ has redeemed us. He has redeemed us completely. That includes our emotions. Now we have the perfect life of Christ and His supernatural power to reflect the emotional beauty of God in our lives. By faith in Christ Jesus, rejoice whenever you have to depend on Him in your emotional life.

Make It Personal

- Do the following exercise as many times as you need. Take a piece of paper. Make three columns. In the first column, write your current circumstances. In the second, write your reactions to what is happening. Be honest and transparent, writing your raw emotions. In the third column, write the truth about God, your circumstances, and your emotions. This is an example from my life:

Circumstances	**Emotions**	**The Truth About God and My Circumstances**
I'm not sleeping well. I have a lot of pain in my back and right ankle. I haven't been able to exercise. I'm surrounded by people all the time, with no break. I have no time to rest with all the things that I have to do for my family.	I feel fear and panic constantly. Thinking about cooking makes me anxious. I don't want to be with people. I want someone to take care of me.	My Father is king (Psalm 97:1) and is bringing about His cosmic plan to reconcile all things through His Son (Ephesians 1:19–20). My life—with its lack of sleep, its pain, and its constant interruptions—has a purpose within that grand plan. All my suffering is preparing me for glory (2 Corinthians 4:17). "God will generously provide all you need. Then you will always have everything you need and plenty left over to share with others" (2 Corinthians 9:8).

- Who defines your identity? (To answer, don't think about who should define it, but where you actually tend to look for your purpose and identity.)
- When you think about God, what is the first thing that comes to mind? Ask that His fatherhood be ever more real and precious to you.
- Start a journal where you can write your prayers and speak to God with complete honesty—not only about your emotions, but also to remember who He is and what His

word tells you. For example, "Lord, I feel anxious about the science test this week. You know all things. You see me. You love me. Please, calm my heart. Keep my thoughts focused on You."

- Can you identify a godly woman in your church you can talk to about your emotions? God designed us to live in community and walk alongside other women who will remind us that truth is a great gift. Reach out to them and try to cultivate a friendship you can be transparent in. Ask them to speak truth to you and confront you when necessary.

EIGHT

God Has Provided Me with a Community So I Can Grow

SUSI BIXBY

"Mom, can I join the group chat? All my friends are in one, and I don't feel connected with them because they talk when they're not in school, and I feel left out." (My daughter said this to me in her first year of middle school.)

"Hey, I'm writing to ask for advice. I have barely any Christian friends, and I feel connected to only my non-believing coworkers. I think that's dangerous, but I don't know what to do because I need to feel that community support somehow." (This is one of the messages that I've received from young women like you.)

Connection. Inclusion. Acceptance. Approval. Support. Community. We all long for these things. We were made to experience them!

Do you believe that? Do you believe your good Creator and Designer wants your emotional and relational needs to be met? Do you believe He has made a way to hold you, encourage you, and help you grow so that you don't have to walk alone?

We've learned how God has provided us with His truth and the means of grace, making our relationships with Him and our perseverance on His path possible. However, there is something key for our lives we still haven't addressed: the church.

The church is kind of strange. Just thinking about church causes mixed reactions in people. There are philosophers who study congregations for social research because there is nothing else like it in society. There are people who observe churches from the outside and form very strong opinions, deciding whether they would participate in something like that.

Others, like me and maybe like you, have been in church for a long time, if not our whole lives. And even then, if we sat in a room and shared our experiences and opinions, we would find a whole range of them.

Are our attitudes toward the church that important? We know we need to read our Bibles, pray, and believe in the gospel and in the truth, but the church is a bit more optional, right?

Do I Need the Church?

I have talked to people who think the church is nothing more than a group of hypocritical sinners, and because of that, it's OK for them to just have their own, private relationship with God. Maybe you've thought that way too at some point. But there is a problem with that way of thinking. While it's true that our relationships with God are personal and individual, that does not mean that God has saved us to let us walk alone. Even though His Word is sufficient for all our needs, that same Word teaches us that the only proper way to walk in the truth is alongside a group of believers, called the "local church."

It may help you—it helped me when I was a teenager—to remember something very important about your original design. Think of the garden of Eden. God created two humans, and He gave them work to do and a purpose to fulfill. But He never wanted them to do it alone. From the beginning, God created Adam and Eve in such a way that they needed each other, and both needed Him. God is honored when we are willing to say "I cannot do it alone." He wants us to recognize our huge and urgent need for Him. And then, as a natural result, we see our great need to walk through this life with other believers.

The Word teaches us that the only proper way to walk in the truth is alongside a group of believers.

Dear friend, you and I need the church.

We need the teaching, the fellowship, the confrontation, the conviction, the encouragement, and the gifts that a local church offers us. I don't know what experiences you've had in churches. You may have grown physically and spiritually alongside a group of people who get along wonderfully and are your extended and beloved family. I also understand that it's possible that your church hasn't always been positive, that you may have been hurt, and that hearing you need the church might confuse you.

There is no perfect church. The reality is that we will all experience some kind of disappointment there. Even though every congregation in this world is full of sinners, it's still essential for every believer—and part of God's beautiful plan—to belong to a local church. The great blessings we find there far outweigh the shortcomings!

What Is the Church?

If I were to approach a group of young people and ask them, "What is the church?" what answers do you think they would give? They would probably say, "It's a building where Christians meet several times a week." Or, "No! It can't be a building. It's a group of people who go to the same place every Sunday and give their offerings. The offering is very important. You aren't part of the church unless you give." "Well, I was told that it's all the believers throughout human history who will one day be in the presence of the Lord."

We must make sure we have a good understanding of what the church is! The church is a group of sinners who have been saved by grace, through Christ's work on their behalf, and who have decided to meet regularly to practice the ordinances (the Lord's Supper and baptism). They walk together in obedience to the Word of God and under the leadership and spiritual care of their pastors.

In other words, *koinonia*.

Sounds strange, doesn't it? Like a name you would get in one of those "discover your *Star Wars* name" games or something.

It's a Greek word from the New Testament that has been used in some churches to teach a biblical concept. I think I understand why it came into use. *Koinonia* means "community," "association," or "fellowship." However, these words, especially *fellowship*, have been poorly understood in some of our churches.

For example, if your pastor speaks of the need to "have fellowship" with brothers and sisters in Christ, what does that mean to you? Pizza and a movie night? Going out to evangelize together? Hanging out after the service to eat? Your answer depends a lot on how things were done in the churches you've attended.

When you think of your church, what words or activities come to mind? *Love, boredom, worship, Bible, conflict, duty, preaching, friends, tithing, religion, service, growth, problems* . . . could be some of them.

Why would someone go to church? Would it be to get something? Do you think every believer should be able to find a church where everything is done according to their preferences? The church is a place we go to so that God will bless us and others will serve us, right?

No! Being part of a church is "having Christ in common" with our brothers and sisters. Christ is the best thing that has happened to our lives, to you and to me and to every person who has received the gift of faith and repentance. So the church is not a spiritual spa service—it's a Christian community where we are encouraged toward love and good works by worshipping the God who saved us (Hebrews 10:24–25). The local congregation God gives us the privilege to participate in is a miracle of His grace and a reflection of His love for us. There is nothing like it on this earth. No other group of people, not even your own biological family, can provide what the church can through Christ.

The local congregation is a miracle of His grace and a reflection of His love for us.

Understanding that any church you and I attend throughout our lives is made up of sinners is crucial. Someone once said that we shouldn't think of the church as a museum where Christ's followers go to display and model their spirituality. We have to think of it as a hospital where needy sinners with serious problems (including me!) go in order to get help from other sinners. In this hospital, we can find the truth preached imperfectly, forgiveness practiced incompletely, and problematic companionship. But all this can glorify God and edify us for His service! And paradoxically, it can be the source of a ton of joy!

Today, most young people expect perfection and believe that a lack of perfection equals hypocrisy. But that's not true, because no one is perfect. We need to be a part of a local body of imperfect believers, and those same shortcomings will contribute to our sanctification. Let's look at what the local church offers and what you so desperately need. You might be surprised.

Why Do I Need the Church?

To help you understand what I mean a little better, here are some different ways you need to view the church and *koinonia* as an indispensable spiritual discipline for standing firm in the truth.

You Need Clear and Frequent Instruction in the Word

You can listen to a whole bunch of podcasts with excellent teaching, read a lot of biblical material online, and read your Bible every day, but that's not enough. You need the preaching of men who are faithful to the Word of God. You need to be surrounded by other young people who know you. They can hold you accountable for what you're learning together, providing you with much encouragement in the ups and downs of your daily life.

The discipline of being alone with the Word and the discipline of listening to it in church meet different needs. They don't work totally separately from each other, but neither one can exist without the other. For example, we can't excuse our absence from church by saying that we've already read the Bible during the week. Hearing the preaching of the Word on Sundays and processing it with other believers will help you understand more when you read it at home, and vice versa. Both practices are necessary and complement each other. There is so much room for growth! There is so much to learn! Don't settle for the idea that you don't need to be taught by others.

You Need to Practice Consistent Obedience Through Faithful Attendance and Participation

What do we do when we go to church? We declare our loyalty and obedience to God! One way of practicing *koinonia* with our brothers and sisters is denying ourselves—and our desires to stay in bed or do something else we like—and going to church. We can encourage other brothers and sisters to do the same. We testify to unbelievers about how much we value God, His Word, and His Church. The church trains me to continually renounce my desires and joyfully obey God by attending, serving, and helping brothers and sisters in need.

I don't want you to get the idea that I wake up every Sunday with an uncontrollable desire to get ready and hurry off to church! I admit that, even though I'm a pastor's wife, some days I don't feel like going. But, without exception, every time I leave church, I ask myself, "What was I thinking?" The joy that the Word of God and fellowship with my brothers and sisters gave me was just what I needed.

Now, let me say something to you from two different points of view. First, as the mother of teenagers, I know that you're already aware that we parents are not perfect. We make mistakes. Sometimes we go to church with bad attitudes. We often don't participate as we should. We get discouraged. We worry about life and neglect what is most important. We need the church the same as you young people do. And seeing a genuine desire and an effort on your part to attend and serve encourages us to keep going. Few things bring more joy to my heart than seeing my children wanting to go to church, worship, listen carefully to the sermon, and fellowship with brothers and sisters. We all need it!

And as a pastor's wife, I can tell you that few things are as encouraging to the leadership of the church as believers who joyfully arrive on time every Sunday to worship and serve at church, showing a genuine interest in the preaching of the Word and giving testimony to the work of God in their lives throughout the week.

Why is this so encouraging? Not only because there are bodies filling the pews, teachers available for the children, more money in the offering, or more open eyes looking at the pastor while he preaches. These things are good and desirable in a certain way. But that's not the point. Brothers and sisters who demonstrate faithfulness in their attendance and joyful participation are living in obedience to God and, in that, glorifying Him. This brings joy to the heart of every pastor and leader because believers are serving with the purpose of glorifying God and seeing His people grow.

Faithfully attending and participating in your church also brings you joy! Since God designed us to enjoy connection and community and worshipping Him, the natural result of obeying Him in these areas is a very special joy. When you are in your church every Sunday, you are joining with the millions of believers who, from generation to generation, have been a part of something much greater than themselves: the advancement of the kingdom of God in this world through the local church.

You Need to Grow in Community

There's a very important word that refers to growth among believers in a local church. I'm sure you've heard of it. *Discipleship*. Maybe you think that discipleship is a twelve-week program that you have to take when you get saved or when you're really rebellious. But discipleship is much, much more. It describes a lifestyle that believers in a local church need to live together!

Koinonia is not always pleasant. We're talking about sinners of different ages, backgrounds, personalities, and weaknesses making up a single body of believers in a local church. The person who thinks they should be free from problems is not being realistic! God uses the constant friction with other redeemed sinners—who are progressing toward the sanctification that they will one day fully experience in their glorified bodies—to reveal the sin that gets in our way. In other words, the members of your local church are instruments chosen by God to help you grow every day.

For you and me to grow in holiness, we need to continuously confess and abandon sin (James 5:16), grow in the knowledge of God and His Word (2 Peter 3:18), cultivate a delight in God's glory (1 Corinthians 10:31), and produce the fruit of the Spirit (Galatians 5:22–23). Discipleship helps in all of these areas! And it happens in the simplest scenarios: informal conversations with a mature friend in the faith, youth group Bible studies, moments of confrontation with an older sister in the faith, or dinner conversations with your parents about questions you have from sermons. We need each other, and frequent discipleship is key to our growth.

The members of your local church are instruments chosen by God to help you grow every day.

You Need the Other Women in Your Local Church

A passage describes the special nature of women's discipleship in the church. Are you familiar with the teaching of Titus 2:3–5? When we study these verses in their broader context (the entire book of Titus), it is truly impressive. God designed the local church so that the relationships between women of different ages contribute to mutual spiritual growth. They help keep young women from blaspheming the gospel and motivate all women to glorify God in their daily lives. It is a key passage for young women in the church.

Many single young women have the impression that this passage doesn't apply to them because it seems to be focused on issues related to married women. Titus 2 describes older women who are mature in the faith investing time and effort into encouraging and instructing younger women with the goal of developing godly character in the context of relationships. It teaches us that we need to train each other to live according to sound doctrine in a practical way.

Marriage and motherhood are not prerequisites for cultivating a life characterized by purity, kindness, self-control, and a love for God's design for the family. Whether God calls you to singleness or to marriage, you need to learn how to be a life-giver to those around you—to the family of faith, to a husband, or to your children.

And if marriage is God's will for you, do you think that a young woman arrives at the altar on her wedding day and all of a sudden becomes someone who wants to be discipled? In order for an older woman to disciple a younger one, the younger woman has to allow herself to be taught. She has to recognize her need for instruction. And I guarantee you—from my own experience—that getting married and having children does not automatically make you "teachable."

As a woman who has arrived at the point in life where I have to admit that I'm now older rather than younger, I can tell you that the young women in my church I have the best "Titus 2" relationship with are those who seek counsel and discipleship from the time they are teenagers. By cultivating a humble spirit that seeks to be taught, they prepare themselves to be that young woman from Titus 2. And the beautiful part is that even while they are still young women, God begins to use them as "older women" to the preteens. Titus 2 is not limited to married women! You need the women in your church, and you can also serve other younger women.

God designed the local church so that the relationships between women of different ages contribute to mutual spiritual growth.

You Need the Gifts of Your Brothers and Sisters in Christ, and They Need Yours

I have heard young women say, "But I don't really have any gifts." Do not believe that lie! Study spiritual gifts in the New Testament (Ephesians 4; 1 Corinthians 12) and spend time in prayer, asking God to help you understand how He works through the gifts of each member.

Gifts are not only about teaching or music. There are also gifts of mercy, generosity, compassion, and service. God has put you in a local body of believers where you may be the ankle or a rib. Without the service and encouragement you can provide, that body is incomplete. Remember that this means that you also need other brothers and sisters. You need to be ministered to by the teaching, encouragement, reproof, and love of others.

But What If I Don't Like My Church?

You may think you can't experience many of the things I'm describing because you don't have a healthy church to attend. I want to help you think for a moment about how to make a decision about church attendance. I understand that many young people from very different situations in life may be reading this book. So instead of presenting specific solutions, I would like to offer you principles you can apply to your situation.

Parental Authority

If you live with your parents, under their care and provision, the Bible commands you to live in obedience and honor toward them (Ephesians 6:1–3). If your parents are believers and go to a church, it's likely that you should accompany them to that church, faithfully and with a good attitude. If your parents are not Christians but allow you to attend church, then you have more freedom to choose. I want to highlight this point of parental authority and the blessing that God promises to children who obey and honor it, because there is

THIS IS

the church

OF THE

living God,

WHICH IS

the pillar

AND

foundation

OF

the truth.

1 TIMOTHY 3:15

a danger for a young woman who begins to analyze the problems in her church and believes that she needs to look for another one.

It is good to grow in discernment and be able to detect errors. It's OK to respectfully approach your parents or leaders and express your concerns. But it's wrong to disobey your parents in regard to attendance or service, or to disrespect them through accusations or criticism. It is better for you to obey God and attend a deficient church under the authority of your parents, trusting in Him to answer your honest and frequent prayers. God is calling you to joyful obedience and submission to your parents and spiritual authorities.

Biblical Requirements as Opposed to Personal Preferences

Have you noticed an exaggerated trend of thinking everything should be done our way? The world shouts a message of self-indulgence in every area of life. If you are a young adult who has the freedom to decide which church to attend for yourself, or a teen whose parents do not take you to church, I'd like to encourage you to look for a church that fulfills biblical requirements rather than your preferences.

If you arrive at a church and the first thing you hear is the music (because that is often the first thing we observe at a new church), try to refrain from immediately reacting, "I can't stand this boring music every Sunday," or "This music is too noisy to be worship; I didn't grow up this way." If you realize that there are no children's classes and they all stay in the main service, don't assume that's a bad thing. If the offering is collected *after* the sermon and not *before*, if the pastor is not wearing a tie or is dressed very formally, if he does not use your preferred version of the Bible—I could go on, but I think you get the point!—pause for a moment, set your preferences aside, and consider the biblical requirements for a local church.

Is the Word preached faithfully—the actual content of the passage and not just a man's ideas? Are the gospel and the person of Jesus Christ at the center of the teaching? This is requirement number one. Why? Because a church that highly values the Word of God and is governed by it is under the protection of the Holy Spirit, who uses the Word in the lives of His people, protecting them from error and producing holiness. You may be able to find many things that aren't done the way you prefer, but those would be secondary.

Faithful Prayer and Sincere Surrender

God wants you to be part of a church that contributes to your spiritual growth and helps you glorify Him. Do you believe this? Then pray fervently, asking for wisdom and guidance. Surrender your desires to God, knowing that He may want you to stay where you are for a while, or go through a season of loneliness, or feel uncomfortable at your church. God can use everything for our good. He asks for faith and surrender. Trust that He is working for your good, your growth, and His glory (Romans 8:28–29).

Beyond just giving you information, I've tried to challenge and encourage you to consider your attitude and perspective toward the church.

- If, up until now, you have seen it as a place to get something, why not begin to pray for God to give you a heart that wants to give and serve?
- If you normally view the church as an obligation or duty, why not ask God for the joy and delight of belonging to a body that has Christ as its head?
- If you have believed that the church is a social club where you spend time only with girls your age, why not pray that God will allow you to develop gospel-filled relationships with older women who are mature in the faith?
- If you are naturally inclined to criticize or become impatient with other brothers and sisters, why not seek to appreciate the gifts of the other members of your local body and begin to pray for their needs?

My young friend, keep listening to truth-centered preachers, and keep reading good articles from blogs like *Revive Our Hearts* and other solid ministries. Keep listening to your favorite Christian podcasts, keep worshipping when you're alone at home by listening to your favorite Christian music, keep enjoying community as part of an online group—and, of course, do all this with discretion!—but do not let yourself miss out on the incomparable blessing of being an active and committed member of a local church!

The church is not an optional track for those who can't handle walking alone. The church is the perfect plan of your redeeming God so that you can enjoy a deeper relationship with Him and your family in the faith. May God help us delight in the wonderful gift that is the church!

Make It Personal

- What has your attitude been toward the church as a general concept and toward your own church specifically? Write down a positive and a negative attitude that you may have detected in your heart while you were reading this chapter.
- Do you truly believe that God is faithful and will provide what

you need, and will do so through the local church where He has placed you?

- Make a list of at least ten blessings and reasons for the joy you can find in your church.
- Do you faithfully participate in listening carefully to the Word, serving alongside your brothers and sisters, and seeking fellowship? If that is not the case, what practical steps should you take to grow in these areas?

NINE

I Need Christ-Honoring Relationships

KELLY NEEDHAM

During the summers of my early college years, I worked for a temping agency. They basically hired me to fill in for employees in different companies who were absent for travel or maternity reasons. My tasks consisted of answering phone calls, greeting clients, organizing files, and entering information into computer forms, among other things. This might seem boring to some people, but I absolutely loved it! Give me tedious, repetitive tasks to accomplish, and I am a happy girl!

One thing I learned from all my bosses was this: As long as I finished the work and did so quickly, they were happy. It didn't matter what I did outside of work as long as I completed the tasks that were assigned to me in the office.

So if I started to go out with my friends every night until one in the morning, my boss wouldn't care as long as it didn't affect my work. If I was dating a boy and started sleeping at his apartment, my boss wouldn't mind as long as it didn't affect my work. If I gained a huge social media following and became addicted to my phone, as long as I was able to get my work done, my boss couldn't care less.

Can I tell you who would care? Can I tell you who would get angry if all these changes started happening in this season of my life? My husband.

It would matter a lot to my husband if I didn't get home to eat dinner with him and instead went out late with my friends. My husband would be very worried if I cultivated a relationship with another man and slept at his house. It would matter a lot to my husband if I were more interested in the attention of strangers on social media than in his attention. All this is important to my husband not because I work for him but because I have a relationship with him—an exclusive, covenant relationship.

This chapter deals with the truth that we need Christ-honoring relationships. So to begin, I want to ask you a question: Why? Why do we need Christ-honoring relationships? Why are our relationships so important to God? Because we don't work for God but rather are in a relationship with Him—an exclusive, covenant relationship.

God is not like our boss. He is like a husband to us. Becoming a Christian is not like starting a new job where we simply have to complete the tasks God assigns us. Becoming a Christian is like getting married; it is entering into an exclusive, covenant relationship with a husband who cares more for your heart for Him and your union with Him than anything else.

We find this marriage-related language throughout the entire Bible. When God spoke of His exiled people through the prophet Isaiah, He said, "Your Creator will be *your husband*; the LORD of Heaven's Armies is his name! He is your Redeemer, the Holy One of Israel, the God of all the earth. For the LORD has called you back from your grief—as though you were a young wife abandoned by her husband," (Isaiah 54:5–6).

The marriage of Hosea, an Old Testament prophet, was converted into a parable of God's message to His people about how He felt about their sins. He was very clear: God sees His people as a husband sees his wife. Listen to the language God uses to describe how He will save His people: "When that day comes, . . . you will call me '*my husband*' instead of 'my master.' . . . I will make you my wife forever, showing you righteousness and justice, unfailing love and compassion. I will be faithful to you and make you mine, and you will finally know me as the LORD" (Hosea 2:16, 19–20).

And just to be crystal clear, the apostle Paul told us explicitly that we are the bride of Christ, that marriage is an earthly shadow of this relationship, and that the actual substance is our union with Jesus: "As the Scriptures say, 'A man leaves his father and mother and is joined to his wife, and the two are united into one.' This is a great mystery, but it is an illustration of the way Christ and the church are one" (Ephesians 5:31–32).

As you read in chapter 4, we were saved for the sole purpose of being in union with God! When Jesus paid for our sins, He did it to save us from the prison of death and bring us to His own house, not just any house. When Jesus lived perfectly for us, he did it to clothe us in white and pure gowns of righteousness so that we might become *His* bride, not the bride of anyone else. When Jesus rose from the dead, He silenced all our accusers and former lovers, demonstrating that He has the eternal power to keep the promises He has made to us as our only true husband.

Why are we raised from death to life by the power of the gospel? Is it only to escape going to hell? Is it only to become better people? No! It's so that we can know Him as a wife knows a husband. So that we can find the fulfillment of joy that comes from being with Him. Peter said, "Christ suffered for our sins once for all time. He never sinned, but he died for sinners *to bring you safely home to God*" (1 Peter 3:18).

We were saved for the sole purpose of being in union with God!

So why do we need Christ-honoring relationships? Because when we are saved by Jesus and begin to follow Him, He becomes our true husband. We do not see Him as a boss who wants us to complete a religious activity. We see Him as a husband who wants our whole hearts and undivided affections. And when our other relationships do not honor Him, we have a big problem.

Order Matters

What types of relationships honor Jesus? How can we be sure that our friendships, work relationships, and all the rest are healthy?

Our relationships may seem very complex. It can be difficult to know what to do in any given situation. Is my friendship unhealthy? Should I end it or keep on going? Should I be this boy's friend or stay away? Should I follow this person on social media? Should I go out with this person from college? How do I connect with people within my business so that I'm honoring Jesus? How do I react when my friend betrays me? Or when those kids at school bully me? Should I have unbelieving friends? What should I do if I feel lonely at church?

It can be very confusing at times! But there is a simple formula we can use to evaluate our relationships and make sure that they are healthy. And we find this formula in Jesus's answer to the question, "Teacher, which is the most important commandment in the law of Moses?" (Matthew 22:36). Now, pay attention to Jesus's answer in the following verses:

> Jesus replied, "'You must love the LORD your God with all your heart, all your soul, and all your mind.' This is the *first* and greatest commandment. A *second* is equally

> important: 'Love your neighbor as yourself.' The entire law and all the demands of the prophets are based on these two commandments." (verses 37–40)

Honoring Christ in relationships is primarily an issue of order. First: Love God with all your heart. Second: Love your neighbor as yourself. And we are in the third and final place. It's all about preserving that order, of standing firm in that truth.

These commandments are like two guardrails on either side of a bridge, keeping us safe as we navigate relationships. We must be sure that loving God is always our first priority, and we must resist our self-centered tendencies, putting ourselves in last place. Healthy, Christ-honoring relationships are always second, never third.

Always Second

Like every good husband, God requires our absolute loyalty. He must always come first. He is not content to share our affections with anyone else. And that is a good thing! How loved would you feel if your husband said to you, "Hey, if you want to cheat on me sometimes, that's okay. As long as you love me like you love the other guy, we're good, right?" Forget it. Who wants a marriage like that? Every good marriage includes a healthy measure of jealousy. It's a sign of deep, mutual devotion.

Healthy, Christ-honoring relationships are always second, never third.

This is why God calls Himself "Jealous." He rightly desires our undivided devotion. In Exodus 34:14, God required His people to destroy all idols, saying, "You must worship no other gods, for the Lord, whose very name is Jealous, is a God who is jealous." Remember that jealousy is not the same as envy. Envy is wanting something that belongs to another. Jealousy is an intolerance for rivals. And God will not tolerate any rivals in our hearts.

So this gives us our first guideline for Christ-honoring relationships in our lives: They must always be second. No other relationship, no matter how significant it is to us, should climb into first place in our hearts. Doing so would dishonor Christ.

Love God with all your heart

and

love your neighbor as yourself.

MATTHEW 22:37–40

We find this theme everywhere in the book of Deuteronomy. Moses spoke to the Israelites before they entered the promised land, and warned them to avoid idolatry. Listen to what he said in Deuteronomy 13:6–10:

> Suppose someone secretly entices you—even your brother, your son or daughter, your beloved wife, or your closest friend—and says, "Let us go worship other gods"—gods that neither you nor your ancestors have known. They might suggest that you worship the gods of peoples who live nearby or who come from the ends of the earth. But do not give in or listen. Have no pity, and do not spare or protect them. You must put them to death! Strike the first blow yourself, and then all the people must join in. Stone the guilty ones to death because they have tried to draw you away from the Lord your God, who rescued you from the land of Egypt, the place of slavery.

God is serious when it comes to having our whole hearts. Don't worry; we are no longer under the law of the Old Testament, so you don't need to go out looking for stones. But the God who spoke these words is the same God we love and serve today. His character never changes. So we can learn something very important from this passage: what God thinks about idolatry and our allowing other things to take His place in our hearts. He won't allow it. It doesn't matter how precious the people are who lead us astray. Even if they are our closest friends, a "friend who is as your own soul" (verse 6 RSV), if they lead us away from God, they become our enemies.

Whose Voice Is the Loudest?

How can we tell whether a relationship has gotten out of order? How can we know that it is no longer secondary and is fighting for God's place? We can begin by asking ourselves, "Who has the loudest voice in my life? Whose authority do I listen to? Whose opinion matters the most? Whose love do I crave most?" If the answer to these questions is anything other than Jesus, then our relationships are out of order.

Let's look at some statements Jesus made to illustrate how other relationships can compete with His voice in our lives. Jesus said, "If you love me, obey my commandments" (John 14:15). So when a relationship consistently causes us to disobey the commandments of God, it has snuck into first place. Here are some examples of what that could look like:

- God asks us to be sexually pure, to reserve all sexual expression for marriage with a man. So if a relationship often tempts us to express our sexuality outside of marriage, God is not first in our lives.
- God asks us to love others selflessly, as we love ourselves. So if anyone in our lives encourages us to hurt others through gossip, bullying, lying, or stealing, God is no longer first in our lives.
- God asks us not to be addicted or enslaved to anything. So if someone in our lives leads us to addiction and we follow them, we have decided that relationship occupies first place. Or if we have become addicted to the presence of a friend, boyfriend, or online friend, and we find that we are unable to spend one day, or even a few hours, without seeing or talking to them, we have allowed them to take first place.

Any relationship in our lives that encourages us to constantly disobey the commands of God is not a relationship we want, at least not in its current form. I don't mean to say that we don't struggle with sin; we all do at times. But a good friend will help us fight sin; they will not make it easy for us to give in to it.

Jesus also said, "If you love your father or mother more than you love me, you are not worthy of being mine; or if you love your son or daughter more than me, you are not worthy of being mine" (Matthew 10:37). Whenever we prefer the love of another above His, that relationship has become too important.

A good friend will help us fight sin; they will not make it easy for us to give in to it.

In a friendship, this means that when you turn to your friend before you turn to Jesus, something is out of place. If you feel you cannot live a single day without your friend, but you can spend weeks without talking to Jesus, that is not healthy. Jesus should be our number one friend, our most important relationship. And this means that all our friendships must take second place. Any friendship that tempts us to move away from Jesus must be dealt with.

The same applies to any other relationship, whether a boyfriend, a boss, or a roommate. If that relationship competes with Jesus for the deepest loyalty of our hearts, it is not OK. If we crave someone's love more than God's, we have a problem of idolatry. At the end of the day, if we are forced to pick sides between Jesus and anyone else, we must always choose Jesus, no matter how this may affect our other relationships. That means that our relationships must always be second.

Yes, the people in our lives are blessings! But allowing these blessings into Jesus's place of greatest honor is idolatry. Anything we give our highest loyalty to that is not God is an idol. The best gift a friend can give us is the commitment to fight for our joy in Christ and for our fellowship with Him. This is why we need Christian friends. We need other people who help us keep Christ in first place and stand firm in the truth.

Never Third

So we know our relationships with other people must never creep into first place. But that doesn't mean we must abandon them. No, we are called to give priority to others and love our neighbors above ourselves. It also doesn't mean that we must isolate ourselves, saying, "As long as I have Jesus, I'm fine." No, it isn't good for us to live alone. We need other people. So while our relationships with others can never be first in our lives, neither can they be last. We must keep them right in the middle, in second place.

This may sound like a simple commandment, but it is extremely difficult to put into practice, because we are self-centered by nature. (Thanks, Adam and Eve!) Our self-centeredness in relationships is often well-hidden in nice activities, subtle, and hard to perceive.

We must look deeper than our actions and begin to assess the motives in our relationships. Why are we so friendly with that person in church? Why are we in that dating relationship? Why are we avoiding that person at work or school? It may seem like we're not doing anything bad, but if our motives are self-centered, it is bad.

In eighth grade, I decided to give all my friends birthday presents like I had never done before. I spent more than usual to celebrate them. But if I'm honest, underneath all that "generosity," I was secretly hoping they would do the same for me and I would receive a lot of attention when my birthday came around. Of course, there is nothing wrong with buying gifts for others! But in my case, I gave only in order to receive something in return. It was selfishness in disguise.

As Christians, it's never OK to use other people to meet our own needs. We are called to put their needs above our own. It's not right for us to choose our friends for any benefits they may bring us. It is not right to be friendly to popular people because they might boost our image. It's not right for us to use social media to fish for compliments or make ourselves look better at someone else's expense. Yes, even online we are called to put ourselves last.

There are thousands of ways we can find ourselves tempted to use another person for our own benefit. So how do we know whether we are doing this in a relationship? Well, let's go back to how Jesus commanded us to love others.

The night before His crucifixion, He said, "Now I am giving you a new commandment: Love each other. Just as I have loved you, you should love each other. Your love for one another will prove to the world that you are my disciples" (John 13:34–35). Jesus calls us to love as He loves us. And how did Jesus love us? By sacrificing Himself for us! He was willing to lose something so that we might gain everything.

Therefore, what must characterize our relationships with others is personal sacrifice. We must be willing to sacrifice our pride, our positions, our popularity, our comfort, and our preferences for the good of others. If we are really putting others second, these types of sacrifices will be present in our lives. So ask yourself, When was the last time you sacrificed something for the sake of someone else?

Loving sacrificially means that we are people who forgive when others fail or betray us. It means we must be servants, willing to take on difficult, unseen tasks. It means we must be evangelists, building friendships with our neighbors, relatives, and colleagues who are not believers, because we want them to know the hope that we have in Jesus. It means we must be merciful, not repaying evil with evil but instead doing good to those who betray us, hurt us, and mistreat us. With the strength God gives us, we put others in second place, praying for both enemies and friends and desiring good for them, not just for ourselves.

No one can love others this way if they haven't put God in first place. Only when we love God daily with all our hearts, our souls, our minds, and our strength will we find the strength to love others selflessly. It is not possible to fulfill this commandment if you haven't fulfilled the first one. So if it all seems overwhelming, start by seeking the Lord and cultivating your relationship with Him. As your heart gives Jesus His proper place, His love will empower you to truly love others.

Where Do We Go from Here?

I don't know anything about your personal situation. It may be that you have godly parents or that you come from a broken home. You may be single or in a relationship. You may have excellent friendships or feel that no one really knows you. Maybe you have been a Christian for a long time or are just starting to learn something about Jesus. Maybe you're finding yourself in the middle of a difficult period of suffering and problems or maybe your life has been great lately.

Even though each of our situations may be very different, Jesus has given us the same commandments: First, love God with everything we have, and second, love others sacrificially. Let's see how this works.

Building strong and healthy relationships that honor Christ begins with a commitment to always put God first. Our daily, number one priority is to delight in the Lord! How can this be achieved? By reading our Bible daily, praying, and attending church with other Christians.

Our daily, number one priority is to delight in the Lord!

If you're not in the habit of reading your Bible and praying daily, this is the first step to take. Pick a time and place to meet with God. Then choose a book of the Bible that you can read in full. Read just one chapter a day, then talk to God about what you learn and write down all the questions you may have. This daily practice of reading the Bible and praying is what God most often uses to speak with us. And don't give up! Persevere. This is not a quick fix but rather the decision to deepen your love for God as a part of your lifestyle.

Secondly, recognize your need to cultivate relationships with other Christians. We need to surround ourselves with flesh and blood people, people who also love Jesus and who can walk with us on our paths in our search for the Lord. It's not enough to have a single good friend. As you read in the previous chapter, we gather in church because we acknowledge that it is good for us to love and worship God in community.

When we're alone, it's easy to give up and become a target for the temptation of sin and fall into idolatry. But together, we will remain steadfast in mutually encouraging each other to seek the Lord and give Him first place! Our inner social circles must be made up of other Christians who can stimulate us to love the Lord and serve others selflessly.

Finally, let's make the daily decision to love others as Jesus loved us. It is not our place to choose who we love this way. First, of course, we will do what He said: Love our *neighbors* as ourselves. Our neighbors are simply the people who are by our sides. Any person who God puts in our paths is someone we are called to love selflessly and to the fullest measure of our abilities. This person may be our classmate, parent, sibling, friend, neighbor, boss, or coworker. Every day we can choose to give preference to others above ourselves.

This sounds like a terrible plan to the world. Who would want to live this way? Putting yourself last? The kingdom of God is truly an upside-down kingdom. It makes no sense for the world. Nonetheless, Jesus assured us that this is the right path:

> If any of you wants to be my follower, you must give up your own way, take up your cross daily, and follow me. If you try to hang on to your life, you will lose it. But if you give up your life for my sake, you will save it. And what do you benefit if you gain the whole world but are yourself lost or destroyed? (Luke 9:23–25)

The way to gain your life is to lose it. The way you can truly thrive is to put yourself last. This is true for all of us who choose to follow Jesus. God first. Others second. Self last. Under this order, we will find life, joy, peace, and flourishing. This is the only way to cultivate Christ-honoring relationships.

Make It Personal

- Which relationship in your life is out of order? Write out a plan to make sure that the relationship is always second, never third, never first.
- What cultural lies might you believe about relationships?
- Do you see God as a boss or as a husband? Are you more concerned with doing things for God or with unreservedly giving Him your heart? How does this idea of God affect your relationships with others? What changes do you need to make in your relationship with God?
- Whose opinion is most important to you? Or, in other words, whose disapproval affects you most? What might this reveal about your heart in that relationship?

- What practical steps must you take in your life to be able to have healthy relationships? (For example, go to a church, pray for Christian friends, have an honest conversation with a friend, confess the sin of idolatry to God in prayer, etc.)

Ten

God Has Designed Me to Be Sexually Pure

KRISTEN CLARK

I still remember the struggle as if it were yesterday. I was a single woman in my twenties and fully aware of my sexual longings and desires. Waiting until marriage to experience sexual pleasure seemed an unreachable goal to me. I knew that God was calling me to defend the purity of my heart, mind, and actions, but I felt it was too difficult. Impossible. Almost like a cruel waiting game. Why would God give me these strong desires as a single woman with no way to express them? With frustration in my heart, I allowed my mind to stray to sinful places. Sexual thoughts invaded my imagination, and when I least expected it, I gave in to carnal self-indulgence . . . again. In those difficult moments, my sexual desires seemed to be more of a curse than a blessing.

If you are struggling with sexual longings and desires, it may be that you are feeling the same things I felt back then. Confusion. Frustration. Discouragement. You may also feel that you are the only Christian girl unable to control her sexual desires. I remember these feelings quite clearly. But as time went by, my eyes were opened to a reality that transformed my life. I was not the only Christian girl in the world who struggled with sexual desires and lust. As I read Christian articles and books on the theme of sexual purity, I realized that sexual desires are part of everyone's experiences and struggles. I also learned that lust was not a problem for teens but rather a human problem. And in the broadest sense, I understood that lust was a matter of sin.

For years, I've worked in a ministry for Christian girls called Girl Defined. And during this time, I have received hundreds of emails from Christian girls asking me to help them address their struggles with sexual sin. Here are some of the things they have written to me:

- "I spend a lot of time struggling with pornography, and I don't know what to do. I'm ashamed, and I'm afraid my secret will become known. I need help, but I can't get it because I'm too ashamed to tell anyone."
- "Lust has been a struggle, both when I am alone and when I am in a romantic relationship."
- "My mind is a war zone. Lust invades my thoughts almost constantly."
- "Lust and purity are subjects that are not often taught about or discussed openly. As a Christian girl, I felt confused and frustrated. We need someone to speak frankly and help us understand what the Bible says on this subject and how we can lead pure lives before the Lord, physically as well as mentally and emotionally."

Everyone, without exception, battles lust and sexual sin. None of us is exempt or immune, whether it is lustful thoughts, pornography, masturbation, sexual promiscuity, an immoral relationship with a man, same-sex desires, or something else, one thing is clear: We, as young Christian women, struggle with sexual sin and impurity.

Everyone, without exception, battles lust and sexual sin.

Instead of casually confronting the struggle with our sin, we must arm ourselves for the battle. When we experience sexual desires and wishes, we must be alert and discern whether our desires honor God or are sinful. Instead of succumbing to our feelings and desires, we should examine them in the light of the Scriptures to discern what is true and right. Regardless of how much we might enjoy doing things our way at any given time, God calls us to honor Him above our desires. It may be that doing things our way is the anthem of our modern culture, but that doesn't lead to a life of integrity or sexual freedom. Indeed, it leads us more and more astray down the path of breakdown and sexual impurity.

Resist the Lies of Our Seductive World

I got into bed and turned on the lamp. It was late. I was tired. But that did not prevent me from reading a romance novel, my favorite literary genre. I justified my actions and convinced myself that these were clean and innocent novels. What harm could they cause? I devoured these novels, one after another. I reread the most erotic scenes over and over. I imagined myself in the characters' shoes, and I imagined that they were my own stories. As a single woman, I imagined that I was the object of the admiration of others, the most sought-after woman.

When the story ended, I stayed in my bed and invented my own story. The fantasies continued in my mind, and I gave free rein to my thoughts. I allowed my mind to wander to places where I knew there was nothing pure or holy.

We live in a time and era when it's considered normal for young women to read novels with a lot of sexual content. We're encouraged to give free rein to our imaginations, to project ourselves onto the sexual experience of another person. The world is more than capable of offering us an unlimited menu of sexually explicit material through books, magazines, and online blogs.

There is also pornography, another level of sexual gratification. We are encouraged to enjoy small doses of pornography as a normal part of our sexual diet. We tell ourselves that it's harmless, that no one will be hurt by it.

On another level, certain real-life relationships and experiences are presented to us things that we should embrace and seek. The world tells us that sexual pleasure should not have any limits. We are free to do what we want with our bodies. Sexting, nude photographs, sleeping with anyone and everyone, and masturbation, among other things, are part of what the world considers fun. According to the world, nothing should be prohibited. Even though this mentality might seem freeing, following the world's ideas for our sexuality and pleasure will never bring us true and lasting satisfaction.

Maria was a young Christian woman who found pornography by accident when she was twelve years old. She saw many images that stuck in her mind. When she became a teenager and had her own phone, she realized she was looking for porn constantly. She tried to stop, but she always wanted to see a little more. It didn't take long before she was addicted to pornography, and she was no longer able to spend even one day without looking at this kind of content. She knew that her actions and desires did not honor the Lord, and she promised herself she would stop doing it. But the tempting seduction of pleasure led her to relapse over and over again. For a while, she felt sincerely guilty, but over time, her conscience was dulled. She stopped reading her Bible and praying. Her heart no longer wished to honor God. She convinced herself that she was free and had freed herself from "Christian moral standards." Sadly, her search for freedom left her more captive and enslaved than she had ever been in her life.

Sin is deceitful because it captures us with seductive promises of pleasure and fulfillment that never last. With the passage of time, the emotion disappears, and we need another dose of sin to continue being happy. When we least suspect it, we are taken captive by our sin and enslaved by its demands. For that reason, 1 Thessalonians 4:3–5 says, "God's will is for you to be holy, so stay away from all sexual sin. Then each of you will control his own body and live in holiness and honor—not in lustful passion like the pagans who do not know God and his ways."

Lasting freedom is not the result of practicing sexual pleasure outside of God's design. True fulfillment cannot be found inside the walls of our own sin. Even though the world glorifies pornography, erotic literature, masturbation, and sexual promiscuity, these things are falsified versions of the holy design God has for sexuality. None of these attractive offers live up to God's glorious plan for genuine sex and intimacy.

As Christian women who live in a world saturated by sex, we must be alert and aware of the seductive lies that surround us. Our goal must always be to discern the difference between genuine, biblical sex and worldly sex, which is a falsification. We must constantly train ourselves to search for the truth. Not every sexual act is in harmony with God's design for sex. Not all sexual practices bring true intimacy to a relationship. Not all sexual acts glorify God. Our primary goal must be to honor and glorify God in all that we do.

Here are three reasons why the worldly version of sexual pleasure doesn't comply with God's overarching design and purpose for sex.

1. Sexual Intimacy Was Created for Marriage

God created sex exclusively for marriage (Hebrews 13:4). Sex was not made for people who are not married. It was created for married relationships. For intimacy. To be shared with a spouse within the marriage covenant. Author Tim Challies notes, "A close examination of the Bible's teaching on sexuality uncovers no reason to believe that God ever intended sex to be a private pursuit. [Genesis 2:23–24; 1 Corinthians 7:2–5; Proverbs 5:18–19; Song of Solomon 1:2–4]. Indeed, the heart and soul of sexuality is the giving and receiving of sexual pleasure between two people—one husband and one wife. Sex is intended to be a means of mutual fulfillment, an expression of love in which a husband thinks foremost of his wife and the wife thinks foremost of her husband."[1]

Most worldly versions of sex (pornography, erotic literature, masturbation, etc.) are completely incapable of serving and giving to the other. The underlying purpose is serving the self. These sinful pleasures lack the relationship-bonding component that God planned for sex. As a result, in light of God's design, these things fall short and do not live up to authentic, holy sex.

We must constantly train ourselves to search for the truth.

2. *Worldly Pleasure Always Feeds on Lust*

Whether single or married, we are all called to cultivate a heart of true purity (see 1 Thessalonians 4:3–5). This includes the search for sexual purity in both our minds and our actions. Practices like masturbation, reading erotic literature, and sexting are driven almost exclusively by impure motives, thoughts, and desires. They lack pure and holy intentions toward God.

Pastor John Piper says, "Sexual desire in itself is good. God made it in the beginning. It has its proper place. But it was made to be governed or regulated or guided by two concerns: honor toward the other person and holiness toward God. Lust is what that sexual desire becomes when that honor and that holiness are missing from it."[2]

Lust is the absence of honor and holiness. It is when we do something to a person, whether in our minds or with our bodies, that does not honor that person. It is allowing our hearts to wander into places that distance us from the holiness of God. As daughters of God, He has called us to seek holiness and purity in our lives, motivated by honor for Him and love of our neighbors. For that reason, Ephesians 5:3 commands us: "Let there be no sexual immorality, impurity, or greed among you. Such sins have no place among God's people."

It is possible for lust and pleasure to be pleasant at the time, but they lack the genuine expression of sexuality that honors God and that His saints are called to.

3. *Sexual Sin Does Not Glorify God*

Within the bond of marriage, sex has the ability to be a beautiful expression of love and worship of God. It is a gift to be enjoyed with gratitude toward the Creator, who made it (see Proverbs 5:18–19). On the other hand, sexual activity outside of marriage does not glorify God because it lacks integrity, purity, and context. Hebrews 13:4 says, "Give honor to marriage, and remain faithful to one another in *marriage*." And 1 Corinthians 6:19–20 reminds us how we must see our bodies: "Don't you realize that your body is the temple of the Holy Spirit, who lives in you and was given to you by God? You do not belong to yourself, for God bought you with a high price. So you must honor God with your body."

When we participate in any sexual activity outside of marriage, we reject God's true design for sex. As a result, we are incapable of glorifying Him with it. Our bodies become vessels of sin instead of vessels of righteousness. Regardless of how intense our sexual impulses and desires may be, glorifying God with your body must be your prime objective. And the gospel means God's power enables you to live this way!

Don't Fall Prey to False Sexuality

Pornography, erotic literature, sexting, masturbation, and premarital sex never succeed in being authentic forms of intimacy that honor God. They cannot tell the story of the love of God that is part of a covenant marriage. They cannot teach us about marital intimacy. They lack the component of sex that binds a relationship from within. They are useless for serving another person unselfishly. They divert our hearts from holiness and purity. And ultimately, they are incapable of glorifying God.

Glorifying God with your body must be your prime objective. And the gospel means God's power enables you to live this way!

Instead of listening to the world's advice or following personal preferences relating to these pleasures that are so popular and attractive, we need to accept God's broader plan for sex and dutifully embrace His design. As hard as this may be, God wants to help us honor Him with how we manage our sexual desires and longings. God wants to help us embrace His beautiful design for sex in the appropriate context for our good and His glory.

The Path to True Purity

If you are currently struggling with some type of sexual sin, I understand the weight and burden this involves. Whether it is pornography, masturbation, erotic literature, sexting, lustful thoughts, or something else, you do not have to fight the battle alone. Galatians 6:2 says, "Share each other's burdens, and in this way obey the law of Christ." God's righteous plan for His daughters is that we help carry each other's our burdens, accompanying each other through trials. Jesus wants your freedom and victory! And it is possible in Him (Romans 6:13–14).

Here are five specific ways you can start to engage in the battle against sexual sin. This advice has helped me throughout my years of struggle with my own sexual sin, and it finally brought me to experience freedom. The list is not exhaustive, but it's a good starting point for your path toward purity that honors Christ.

1. Seek True Repentance

The first step toward victory over sexual sin is recognizing that we have sinned against God and that we need His forgiveness. 1 John 1:9 says, "If we confess our sins to him, he is faithful and just to forgive us our sins and to cleanse us from all wickedness." Our God is full of grace and forgiveness and wants to receive and forgive any person who seeks Him with a sincere heart.

2. Ask for God's Help Every Day

Instead of counting on our own strength to battle against sin, we must remember that although we have many limitations, God is offering everything we are lacking. Because the power of Christ works within us, we can live a life free from the control of sexual sin. Romans 6:11 reminds us, "You also should consider yourselves to be dead to the power of sin and alive to God through Christ Jesus." The priority in our lives and in our battles against sin must be to seek God's help through prayer every day.

3. Bring Secret Sins into the Light

Sexual sin flourishes in the darkness. There is something powerfully liberating about bringing secret sins into the light. Proverbs 28:13 says, "People who conceal their sins will not prosper, but if they confess and turn from them, they will receive mercy." God promises to extend His mercy to us if we bring our sexual sin into the light. Whether it be pornography, masturbation, erotic literature, or any other kind, if you truly want freedom, ask God to grant you the courage to bring it into the light by confessing your struggle to a godly woman.

4. Seek the Constant Discipleship of a Godly Woman

After bringing your sexual battle into the light, don't shut yourself up in your private world again. Breaking sinful habits is hard work. Don't fight your battles alone, isolated from others. Approach a godly woman you know and ask her to instruct you in God's truth. Depending on the nature of your specific struggle (i.e., pornography, masturbation, erotic literature, sexting, etc.), think about what Bible-centered book you could read on the subject. You could also pray together every week. She could provide you with an "open door" in terms of accountability so you can call her or send her a text message each time you feel tempted to relapse in your sexual battle.

5. Make Radical Changes

Depending on the frequency and seriousness of your sexual battle, you may need to make some radical changes in your life in order to prevent relapses and sin. For example, if you are struggling with pornography, consider using your phone or computer only in public places, installing a serious internet-monitoring program, or taking a technology break for a while. If you are struggling with erotic literature, take the initiative to get rid of those books and movies, erase any erotic content from your electronic devices, and avoid using your devices when you're alone. If you are struggling with masturbation, assess which places present you with the most temptation. It may be your room, in the shower, or when you are tired. Design a plan of action ahead of time to determine how you are going to manage these temptations when they come.

It's my prayer that you take these five recommendations seriously, and that you start on your path toward sexual freedom today. As someone has beautifully reminded me, "In order to duly embrace our sexuality, we must submit it to He who created it. When we do this, we do not fight against our sexuality but rather we fight for it. We rescue our sexuality from the claws of lust. We exalt our identity given by God as sexual creatures who refuse to become prisoners to the insatiable discontent of lust."

Single Young Woman, You Were Created for True Intimacy

It was three weeks before my wedding day. I was eager to finally marry the man I had promised to give my life and my love to. My longings for lifelong marriage, intimacy, and companionship were finally going to come true. As the big day approached, my love for Zack, my future husband, had grown deeper and deeper. I longed for the moment I would finally be his. I longed to give him my whole being. I longed for us to finally be *one*.

Perhaps you also feel that profound desire for companionship, unity, and intimacy in your life. Perhaps you have felt an inner longing to be fully known,

For
this
is
the will
of God,
your
sanctification.

1 THESSALONIANS 4:3 RSV

valued, and deeply loved by someone. From the moment your sexual desires awoke, it's likely you have also felt an intense drive for sexual satisfaction and fulfillment. It is a normal part of being human. Everyone experiences it! But I have wonderful news for you. You do not have to be married to understand how to embrace God's wondrous plan for intimacy. Even though you may be young, the sexual desires and wishes God has given you serve to teach you wonderful truths about God Himself. As you begin to understand a true biblical perspective on sex, you will begin to realize that sex is not the final goal. The final goal is having a deep, intimate, and fulfilling relationship with God.

God designed sex and intimacy as an earthly metaphor for a much greater spiritual reality. Throughout the Bible, God used a very specific Hebrew word to help us understand His intimate love for us. The word is *yada*. It "implies a deep, personal, and relational knowledge."[3] Sexual intimacy between a husband and wife is an earthly metaphor for God's desire to know each one of us deeply.

God designed sex and intimacy as an earthly metaphor for a much greater spiritual reality.

When I learned about the word *yada* for the first time, I was completely stunned. How wonderful to know that God uses the same word (*yada*) to describe both His relationship with me and the sexual intimacy between a husband and wife. Single women do not need to wait until marriage to experience *yada* in its maximum expression, which is to know God deeply. He created you so that you may be known intimately and so that you may know Him deeply. He wants to have an intimate relationship with you right now.

When we take a step back and look at the most complete picture of sex in the context of the Bible, we begin to see that sex is nothing more than a metaphor that points to what truly matters: the profound love of God for His children. The most satisfactory experience we can seek is not an amazing sexual adventure, but rather an authentic relationship with Jesus.

The next time you feel a sexual impulse or ask yourself if you will ever experience sexual intimacy, allow these moments to remind you that your true need is a relationship with Jesus. Channel your longings to bring you to a deeper knowledge of Christ and find ultimate satisfaction in Him. The more you understand the heart of God for sex and intimacy, the more you will understand that He is not depriving you of anything—quite the opposite. He is offering you true intimacy now by means of a genuine relationship with Him. I love the words of Psalm 139 that say,

> O Lord, you have examined my heart
> and know everything about me [*yada*]. . . .
>
> You made all the delicate, inner parts of my body
> and knit me together in my mother's womb.
> Thank you for making me so wonderfully complex!
> Your workmanship is marvelous—how well I know
> [*yada*] it.
>
> (verses 1, 13–14)

I want to challenge you to escape the worldly mold for sexuality and, starting today, to adopt a true, biblical vision of sexuality. Don't wait until you have a romantic relationship or until you are engaged or married. Start on this path right away, today. Single women are sexual beings just like other people. God has a good plan for you. Your sexual desires were never designed to be the true source of fulfillment in your life. You were created for an amazing God who loves you and wants to have an intimate, covenant relationship with you. He wants to know you (*yada*) deeply and love you more fully than any human ever could. His covenant love is what your soul really needs. When you experience sexual longings, desires, and temptations in your daily life, my prayer is that all of it will remind you that you were created for something bigger, for Someone bigger.

God is looking out for you and has a good and beautiful plan for your sexuality. He wants to help you find true freedom as you seek to put His good design for your life into practice.

Make It Personal

- What has most influenced your life in forming your current perspective of sexuality?
- How have you felt alone in your struggles with sexual sin?
- Take a moment to speak frankly. What battles with lust have you faced, and should they be brought into the light?
- Your path to sexual freedom can begin today. Of the following five recommendations, which ones do you need to put into practice?

- Seek true repentance.
- Ask for God's help every day.
- Bring secret sins into the light.
- Seek the constant discipleship of a godly woman.
- Make radical changes.

- Why is a genuine relationship with Jesus even more important and powerful than a sexual relationship?

ELEVEN

God Will Not Fail Me

The Promises of God and Eternity in Our Hearts

ERIN DAVIS

My plan was to discourage any attempt at conversation, but the neighboring passenger in seat 12 didn't catch on. I was traveling alone. In those situations, I usually put on my headphones and immerse myself in reading instead of making new friends with strangers. However, the woman who sat beside me wanted to talk. I will never forget our conversation.

As the flight went on, she told me a heartbreaking story of loss. She had suffered more than most of us ever will. When she finished telling me her story and dried her tears, I felt a lump in my throat. I didn't know what to say. Finally, I managed to ask, "Are God's promises true?"

She smiled at me and whispered, "Every one of them."

That day, a stranger gave me an amazing gift: hope in the true promises of God. I hope to put that gift in your hands with this chapter. If our questions about the future look like an ocean of roiling waves, God's promises are our lifeboat.

BETTER THAN A CRYSTAL BALL

When you think about the future, I know that you have questions to ask. We all do. Maybe you ask yourself . . .

- Will I get married? If I get married, who will I marry?
- Will I have children? If so, how many will I have?
- What career does God want me to pursue?
- What college should I attend?
- Will I have the house of my dreams?
- Will I have the same friends? Will I make new friends?
- Will I be happy?
- Will I enjoy good health?

God has decided not to give us a crystal ball. None of us know what tomorrow will bring, nor the next month, nor the next year. However, that doesn't mean we must walk blindly into the future. God has given us something much better than a crystal ball. He's given us His promises! We can't know every detail of how our lives are going to turn out, but we can rest easy in the certainty that God has promised us a bright future. I'm going to present five promises from the Word of God, and I pray they transform the way you feel about your future. I've written them in the first person to help you internalize them. In fact, why not take a Post-it note and write them down? Then put it in a place where you can see it frequently (like on your bathroom mirror or nightstand) and remember God's promises.

God's promises are our lifeboat.

Promise #1: God Isn't Going to Change His Opinion of Me

Hebrews 13:8 promises that "Jesus Christ *is* the same yesterday, today, and forever."

Jesus does not change. The Jesus of the beginning of time is the same as today. *And the Jesus of today will be the same in the future.* His love for you does not change. He has described it as an "everlasting love" (Jeremiah 31:3). It's a love that is and that will be—forever.

No matter what the future holds for you, no matter what mistakes you make, no matter what sins you will fall into, and no matter what successes or failures await you, *God is not going to change His opinion about you.* His love for you doesn't deplete as the years go by. You can count on His eternal love being with you in every step of your life.

Promise #2: God Will Never Leave Me

It's probable that the future holds some disappointment for you. That is part of what it means to live in a fallen world. It could be that some friendships will end badly. It could be that some relationships that are important to you now will weaken in the future. But you have a friend you can count on to be present in each and every moment of your life: Jesus Christ.

Maybe you've heard the powerful message God sent to Joshua with words of great inspiration!

> Be strong and courageous! Do not be afraid and do not panic before them. For the Lord your God will personally go ahead of you. He will neither fail you nor abandon you. (Deuteronomy 31:6)

When we read the whole story, we see that Joshua was facing an uncertain future. He was about to assume the position of leadership previously occupied by Moses.

Would the people respect his leadership?

Was he a strong enough leader to take them to the promised land?

What would their lives be like when they arrived?

While Joshua didn't have all the answers, he had a promise that he could count on. God would never, ever leave him nor fail him.

We have the same promise. Listen to what Jesus tells us.

> I am with you always, even to the end of the age. (Matthew 28:20)

He will be with us always and forever. No matter what awaits us in the future, we can be sure that Jesus will be there.

Promise #3: My Future Will Be Amazing!

I don't have the answers to your list of questions about the future, but I do know that your future (and mine!) is more wonderful, satisfying, and amazing than our hearts could ever dream of.

Listen to what awaits all those who have surrendered their lives to Jesus:

> Then I saw a new heaven and a new earth, for the old heaven and the old earth had disappeared. And the sea was also gone. And I saw the holy city, the new Jerusalem, coming down from God out of heaven like a bride beautifully dressed for her husband.
>
> I heard a loud shout from the throne, saying, "Look, God's home is now among his people! He will live with them, and they will be his people. God himself will be

> with them. He will wipe every tear from their eyes, and there will be no more death or sorrow or crying or pain. All these things are gone forever." (Revelation 21:1–4)

The future for all who believe is an eternity with Jesus. All that disturbs us today and all that will disappoint us tomorrow are destined to disappear. Our presents may be filled with "all these things," but this isn't for long; these things will pass. Our life with Jesus will be free from tears, death, grief, and pain.

What a great promise!

No matter what awaits us in the future, we can be sure that Jesus will be there.

Promise #4: Everything Works Together for My Good

I encourage you to memorize Romans 8:28. The verse says, "We know that God causes everything to work together for the good of those who love God and are called according to *his* purpose for them."

God is going to use everything that happens in your life—yes, *everything*—for your good and His glory. When we ask ourselves about the future, what we really mean is, "Is everything going to go well?" The answer, thanks to Jesus, is yes!

Under God's sovereign care, every moment of our lives is redeemed. The good and the bad are woven together in the tapestry that is God's plan for us, and in the end, the result will be truly beautiful.

Maybe you don't know what the future holds for you, but you do know that, come what may, God has promised to redeem it for your good.

Promise #5: God Will Not Fail Me

I have four sons. When they have a difficult day or our family is going through hard times, I've developed the habit of looking into their eyes and asking, "Will God fail us this time?"

They've already been through this enough times to know the answer: "No, Mommy."

Listen to what Joshua 21:45 says: "Not a single one of all the good promises the Lord had given to the family of Israel was left unfulfilled; everything he had spoken came true."

Practice repeating this with me:

"God's promises will not fail."

"God's promises will not fail."

"God's promises will not fail."

In 1 Thessalonians 5:24, Paul reminded us, "God will make *this* happen, for he who calls you is faithful."

If God has promised you something, you can be sure of it. He is not going to go back on His word. He will always, always fulfill His Word.

When life appears to have more questions than answers, you can know that God will not fail you.

When your future doesn't turn out like you hoped, you can know that God will not fail you.

When your dreams don't come true the way you had imagined, you can know that God will not fail you.

Taking refuge in the promises of God means that we can dare to ask, "Will God fail us this time?" and remain confident that the answer will always be no.

Our God and the Roll of Paper

We take refuge not only in God's promises but also in the character of God. When we think about our futures, we take particular encouragement in the fact that God is already there.

One of the most wondrous aspects of God is His omnipresence. He is everywhere at the same time. He is with you at this very moment and also here with me on my sheep ranch in Missouri. He is down in Antarctica and as far north as the North Pole. His omnipresence also means that He is with us at this moment while also already existing in the future. He is in you here and now and in you later. There is no moment of your life in which God is not present.

Listen to how God describes Himself in Revelation 1:8: "I am the Alpha and the Omega—the beginning and the end. . . . I am the one who is, who always was, and who is still to come—the Almighty One."

He is the God that is.

He is the God that was.

He is the God that is to come.

The omnipresence of God can be too big of an idea for my tiny brain, so I like to imagine that God is like a roll of paper. I can take a roll of paper and see it from beginning to end. So it is for God with me. He created time but is outside of it. He holds your entire life in His hands, every second of it, and He sees it from beginning to end. That is huge! He is wondrous!

There are too many things that we cannot know about our futures, but we can be confident in what we don't know about *ourselves* thanks to all that we already know about *Him*.

A Future Without Fear

How can we live in light of these beautiful promises and the admirable character of God? Here are three decisions that we can make.

Decision #1: I Will Trust That I Have All I Need

In 2 Peter 1:3, we read, "By his divine power, God has given us everything we need for living a godly life. We have received all of this by coming to know him, the one who called us to himself by means of his marvelous glory and excellence."

You can worry about the future. You can worry that it won't be what you hope. You can spend time striving so that everything comes out just how you want it, or you can trust that the Word of God is the truth and that you have all you need to live the life He has provided for you, both in the present and in the future.

Decision #2: I Can Face the Future Without Fear

Let's look back over the promises I've already mentioned.

- Promise #1: God isn't going to change His opinion of me.
- Promise #2: God will never leave me.
- Promise #3: My future will be amazing!
- Promise #4: Everything works together for my good.
- Promise #5: God will not fail me.

Do you believe these promises are true? If you answered yes, thank God for the faith He has given you. If you answered no, stop here and ask the Lord to help you with your disbelief. Because these promises truly change how we deal with the future.

If God will be with us regardless of the circumstances—if He's already seen our pasts, our presents, and our futures—if His promises cannot fail—then we can face our futures without fear. What freedom!

Decision #3: I Can Prepare for My Future Starting Now

In the end, our future is with Christ, worshipping Him for eternity. That may seem like a distant reality, but this is not the case in the grand scheme of things. The best way to be ready for our ultimate future is to start preparing for it now.

- Do you spend your days worshipping Jesus?
- Do you dedicate time for contemplating Him through the lens of His Word?

And we know
that God causes
everything to

WORK TOGETHER
FOR THE GOOD
OF THOSE
WHO LOVE GOD

and are called
according to
his purpose for them.

ROMANS 8:28

- Are you engaged in serving the church?

The best preparation for a future with Him is living in light of eternity from this very moment onward.

Hearts Made for Eternity

God has designed us to ask questions about the future, but maybe not in the way that you think.

Ecclesiastes 3:11 says, "God has made everything beautiful for its own time. *He has planted eternity in the human heart,* but even so, people cannot see the whole scope of God's work from beginning to end."

Your heart was made to focus on eternity, not to get wrapped up in the here and now. I love the way that Jonathan Edwards expressed this truth. He frequently prayed, "Lord, stamp eternity on my eyeballs."

Your heart was made to focus on eternity, not to get wrapped up in the here and now.

Yes, you have a future. That future could include going to college or not, or having your dream job or not. It could be that you get married to the man of your dreams, or not. It could include a house full of children, or not even one. Getting fixated on that type of outcome is only going to lead to more questions. However, your ultimate future is decided: You are going to be with Jesus forever. When your heart is bursting with questions about your future, learn to pray, "Jesus, stamp eternity on my eyeballs."

I don't have a crystal ball. I can't predict the future. But if you ask me whether God's promises are true, I have no doubt at all about the answer.

They are. Every. Single. One of them.

Make It Personal

- Which uncertainties about the future cause you the most anxiety?
- Which of God's five promises covered in this chapter encourage you the most? Why?

- How do you imagine your future with Jesus? Write about it or draw a picture to express your answer.
- In your opinion, what does it mean that God has put eternity in our hearts? How have you seen this in your own life?
- What are your deepest desires for the future?

Conclusion

A Challenge for You

BETSY GÓMEZ

Thanks for making it this far! I can't tell you how much I hope that God has filled your heart with conviction about the importance of the truth of His Word—and that you are ready to surrender completely to His will, no matter the cost. If I could, I'd jump right out of these pages, look you in the eyes, and beg you not to let what you've read get pushed to the back of your mind.

I say that because, when you least expect it, the world will hit you with a wave that will try to drag you to destruction. The Enemy will use all his tricks to bring you down, and your sin will try to seduce you. So, what will you do? How will you respond to the pressure?

I want to challenge you to do two things that might seem impossible: Be strong and stand firm. If someone had told my younger self to be strong and stand firm, I probably would have said, "You don't understand! I've tried, but I just can't! No matter what I do, I keep falling."

I know that I can't fully understand what it's like to be your age right now—to stand firm in your faith at school, work, or wherever you are. I don't know your friends or the environment you have to deal with. I can't imagine how complicated it can be to stand firm under the pressure you're experiencing. However, there is something I do know. I know how hard it is to keep trying to fight with the wrong strength and weapons. I tried to stand firm, but I was growing tired and frustrated. I felt so powerless! So, if until now you've been trying without success, I want to invite you to change your strategy.

Believe it or not, you can be strong and stand firm in the truth! In fact, this is the same call Paul made to the believers in Ephesus. His command can be found in a biblical passage you've probably read or at least heard. It's in Ephesians 6:10–17. Look it up in your Bible and read it. I'll wait here. (No cheating!)

It's the famous passage that mentions the armor of God. In these verses, there are two key commands. Can you identify them? Here, I'll give you two clues. One is found in verse 10 and the other in various verses, but it's especially clear in verse 11. Try to find them.

Yes! That is exactly what I am asking you to do. Be strong and stand firm.

Be Strong

> A final word: Be strong in the Lord and in his mighty power. (Ephesians 6:10)

Being strong isn't optional. We have been called to a battle that requires a lot of strength. And maybe you're thinking, "You see? I'm not qualified, because I'm not strong!" I have good news for you: That is precisely why you're qualified!

When we try to look to ourselves for the strength we need to stand firm, we end up frustrated because we fall short. We're weak. Our faith wavers. Our love is fragile. We get tired and fall. And that's exactly what we need to realize. We are weak when we live according to our own strength!

Stop searching for your strength in the wrong places. You're not going to find it in your abilities or your talents. It's not even in the years you've spent serving the church or the ministries you belong to. You won't find it in the opinions of the crowds or in the advice of your "super spiritual" friends.

The key to being strong is found in knowing the right source of power. Christ is strong, and the strength we need to stand firm before the tricks of the Enemy is found in His power. The command is clear: "Be strong in the Lord and in his mighty power." The world keeps telling you that you're strong on your own and has sold you a false idea of empowerment. Don't believe it! You are weaker than you can imagine, but if you are in Christ, He is strong in you. You are united with Christ, and in Him you have all the power you need to overcome.

In the midst of temptation, when you feel everything in you is making you believe that sin will satisfy you more than God, instead of looking at yourself and seeing how weak you are, look to Christ. He is strong enough to sustain you. He can be relied on to save you in your time of weakness. His grace will always be stronger than your sin. That is the moment to tell your soul, "Yes, I am weak, but I am united with Christ. In Him I am strong!"

Do you see? In God's math, the weak are the strong. So be strong through the grace God gives you in Christ Jesus![1] Being strong in Him shows up when you walk with Him each day—when you seek to know and do His will, and when you pray that through His Spirit, He will help you take on the promises that give you the upper hand against any temptation or sin.

Believe, by faith, that the strength you need to stand firm is found only in Him. And when I say "believe by faith," I mean that you can renounce what seems so attractive now, through the love of Christ, who promises you greater satisfaction.

Stand Firm

> Put on all of God's armor so that you will be able to stand firm against all strategies of the devil. (Ephesians 6:11)

God is so generous that when He calls us to do something, He equips us with all we need to achieve it. He calls us to be strong and gives us strength through our union with Christ. He also calls us to stand firm against the attacks of the Enemy, and He provides us with all that we need: the armor of God.

That said, have you ever asked yourself how it works? Or how to put on the armor of God? I admit, I had no idea of the real meaning of these verses.

I remember that in VBS, we put together dance routines in which we put on the armor, and at the end, we sang at the top of our lungs that we were soldiers ready to win the battle of faith. I used to think putting on the armor of God worked like Iron Man's suit—just call for it, and suddenly you are invincible.

A few years later, before leaving home, I would look at myself in the mirror and recite Ephesians 6:11–17 while mentally "putting on the armor." I thought that just declaring it to the spiritual world would make the hordes of evil flee and prevent them from attacking me.

But something was wrong, because this "effect" of my armor didn't last long. There was no connection between the pieces of the armor and the sin I was falling into over and over again. And I didn't know how to connect them with the conflicts I ended up in because of my disobedience. And I finally asked myself, "How is this kind of ritual going to help me stand firm? How is the armor of God supposed to work?"

I loved listening to the sermon by pastor Tony Merida on how Ephesians 6 "is about putting on the characteristics and virtues that are ours through our union with Jesus Christ. We must be clothed with Christ, as Ephesians 4:24

['put on your new nature, created to be *like God*—truly righteous and holy'] says, which simply means recognizing who you are in Christ and living in accordance with that identity with your own spiritual resources."[2]

That is what you need to stand firm: "Recognizing who you are in Christ and living in accordance with that identity with your own spiritual resources."

Putting on the full armor of God is using what He has provided to defeat the Enemy: the gospel. There we can find all the power and resources we need to stand firm. We can "dress ourselves" with the truth that we have been saved.

You see? It's much easier to look at ourselves in the mirror and say, "I'm putting on the armor of God" like a spiritual mantra than it is to snuff out the sin in ourselves and stand firm in the truth of the gospel. It requires us to be completely dependent on God and His Word. And we should take great encouragement from Paul's calling the whole church to this. It's something that we can't do alone! We stand firm by being united in Christ and His body, the church.

At this point you might think, "Fine, but how do I put this into practice Sunday through Saturday, when my emotions betray me and when I feel tempted to fall into a sin that constantly tries to seduce me?"

- **Stand firm in the truth of Christ,** putting on the belt of truth. Eliminate all lies or deceitfulness from your mind and your mouth. Call out the lies in your heart, your words, and your life. Reject it all and put on the truth of Christ. The Enemy is the Father of Lies, so defend your position with the truth of Christ.
- **Stand firm in doing what is right,** putting on the breastplate of righteousness. Snuff out all evil deeds (simply by not feeding the sin that drives you to do what is wrong). Clothe yourself with the justice that characterizes Christ; in Him, you have the power to live in obedience to God.
- **Stand firm in proclaiming the gospel,** putting on the shoes of peace. Wherever you go, be a messenger of the good news that Christ came to the world so that humanity could be at peace with God. Don't stay silent!
- **Stand firm in faith,** holding up the shield of faith. Saturate your mind with the truth so that lies can't take hold. Identify the lies that are hidden in the attacks of the Enemy and quiet them with the truth of God's Word.
- **Stand firm in the security of your salvation,** putting on the helmet of salvation. Christ saved you for good, and nothing and

no one can separate you from Him! Take up that truth when you feel doubt and fear wanting to cut you down.

- **Stand firm in the Word of God,** taking the sword of the Spirit. Jesus defeated Satan in the desert by responding with the Word of God. So you can also stand firm against temptation, fill yourself with His truth.

When everything within you is screaming lies, remember who you are in Christ and believe in it. Bear in mind that you are loved, chosen, and forgiven; you are united with Christ, His victory is yours, and in Him, you will find all the grace that you need to stand firm. Use everything God has given you in Christ. Every single day.

Remember, believe, and live the gospel by faith. Every day.

Young true woman, stand firm in the Truth. Stand firm in Christ!

PART 3

Join the Movement

APPENDIX A

Join the Young True Woman Movement!

BETSY GÓMEZ

Young True Woman calls on young women to embrace the truth that will free them from the lies of the world, culture, and society, to cherish Christ above all things, and to live in such a way that the beauty of the gospel shines before those around them.

A YOUNG TRUE WOMAN . . .

1. Renews her mind and bases her walk on the Word of God; this is her delight and constant meditation.

> Don't copy the behavior and customs of this world, but let God transform you into a new person by changing the way you think. Then you will learn to know God's will for you, which is good and pleasing and perfect. (Romans 12:2)

> Oh, how I love your instructions!
> I think about them all day long.
> (Psalm 119:97)

2. Recognizes that God is her supreme authority; therefore, all her relationships are characterized by submission.

> For the Lord is God,
> and he created the heavens and earth
> and put everything in place.
> He made the world to be lived in,
> not to be a place of empty chaos.
> "I am the Lord," he says,
> "and there is no other."
> (Isaiah 45:18)

> In the same way, you who are younger must accept the authority of the elders. And all of you, dress yourselves in humility as you relate to one another, for
>
> "God opposes the proud
> but gives grace to the humble."
> (1 Peter 5:5)

3. Accepts her design with joy and surrenders voluntarily to the purpose God has for her life.

> Then God looked over all he had made, and he saw that it was very good! (Genesis 1:31)

> Dear brothers and sisters, I plead with you to give your bodies to God because of all he has done for you. Let them be a living and holy sacrifice—the kind he will find acceptable. This is truly the way to worship him. (Romans 12:1)

4. Has been cleansed of sin and finds the power to live in purity and holiness in the gospel.

> Anyone who belongs to Christ has become a new person. The old life is gone; a new life has begun! (2 Corinthians 5:17)

> I am not ashamed of this Good News about Christ. It is the power of God at work, saving everyone who believes—the Jew first and also the Gentile. (Romans 1:16)

5. Has her eyes on the things of heaven, where Christ is, and places all her hope in the eternal joy that He has promised.

> Since you have been raised to new life with Christ, set your sights on the realities of heaven, where Christ sits in the place of honor at God's right hand. Think about the things of heaven, not the things of earth. For you died to this life, and your real life is hidden with Christ in God. (Colossians 3:1–3)

Join the movement! Be a young true woman and call others to the freedom, fullness, and fruitfulness that can be found only in Christ.

APPENDIX B

The True Woman Manifesto

We believe that God is the sovereign Lord of the universe and the Creator of life, and that all creation exists for His delight and to bring Him glory (1 Corinthians 8:6; Colossians 1:16; Revelation 4:11).

We believe that the creation of humanity, as man and woman, was a deliberate and wonderful part of God's wise plan, and that men and women were created to reflect the image of God in complementary but distinct forms (Genesis 1:26–27; 2:18; 1 Corinthians 11:8).

We believe that sin has separated all humans from God and has made us unable to reflect His image as we were created to do. Our only hope of restoration and salvation lies in repenting of our sins and trusting in Christ, who lived a life without sin, died in our place, and was raised from the dead (Genesis 3:1–7, 15–16; Mark 1:15; 1 Corinthians 15:1–4).

We recognize that we live in a culture that neither acknowledges God's right to reign nor accepts the Scriptures as the standard for living life, and is suffering the consequences of abandoning the design God has for men and women (Proverbs 14:12; Jeremiah 17:9; Romans 3:18; 8:6–7; 2 Timothy 3:16).

We believe that Jesus Christ is redeeming this sinful world and making all things new. And His followers are called to share His redemptive purpose as they seek, through His power, to transform those aspects of life that have been sullied and ruined through sin (Ephesians 4:22–24; Colossians 3:12–14; Titus 2:14).

As Christian women, we want to honor God by living countercultural lives that reflect the beauty of Christ and His gospel to the world.

To This End, We Declare That . . .

The Scriptures are the medium, authorized by God, that instructs us in His ways and reveals His design for our femininity, characters, priorities, roles, responsibilities, and relationships (Joshua 1:8; 2 Timothy 3:16; 2 Peter 1:20–21; 3:15–16).

We glorify God and experience His blessings when we accept and joyfully embrace His design, functions, and order for our lives (1 Timothy 2:9; Titus 2:3–5; 1 Peter 3:3–6).

As redeemed sinners, we cannot fully express the beauty of our biblical femininity while separated from the sacred work of the gospel and the power of the Holy Spirit that dwells in us (John 15:1–5; 1 Corinthians 15:10; Ephesians 2:8–10; Philippians 2:12–13).

Both men and women were created in the image of God and are equal in value and dignity but have distinct roles and functions in the home and in the church (Genesis 1:26–28; 2:18; Galatians 3:26–28; Ephesians 5:22–33).

We are called, as women, to affirm and encourage men in their search to express their biblical masculinity, and to honor and support the leadership that God has ordained them in the home and in the church (Mark 9:35; 10:42–45; Genesis 2:18; 1 Peter 5:1–4; 1 Corinthians 14:34; 1 Timothy 2:12–3:7).

Marriage, as created by God, is a sacred pact, binding until death, between a man and a woman (Genesis 2:24; Mark 10:7–9).

When we respond with humility to masculine leadership, in the home and in the church, we show a noble submission to authority that reflects the submission of Christ to the authority of God, His Father (Ephesians 5:22–33; 1 Corinthians 11:3).

Selfish insistence to assert our personal rights is contrary to the spirit of Christ, who humbled Himself, taking the form of a servant and delivering His life to us (Luke 13:30; John 15:13; Ephesians 4:32; Philippians 2:5–8).

Human life is precious to God and must be appreciated and protected from the moment of conception until death (Psalm 139:13–16).

Children are a blessing from God, and women were especially designed to be givers and sustainers of life, whether their children are biological or adopted, and to be so to other children in their spheres of influence (Genesis 1:28; 9:1; Psalm 127; Titus 2:4–5).

God's plan for humanity goes beyond marriage. All women, married or single, must exhibit femininity in their varied relationships, displaying a distinct modesty, sensitivity, and gentleness of spirit (1 Corinthians 11:2–16; 1 Timothy 2:9–13).

Suffering is the inevitable reality of a fallen world. Sometimes we will be called on to suffer when we do what is right, and to look to heavenly reward over earthly delights, for the good of the gospel and the advancement of Christ's kingdom (Matthew 5:10–12; 2 Corinthians 4:17; James 1:12; 1 Peter 2:21–23; 3:14–17; 4:14).

Mature Christian women have a responsibility to leave a legacy of faith, discipling young women in the Word and the ways of God and shaping a life of fruitful femininity for the next generation (Titus 2:3–5).

Believing What Was Previously Said . . .

We declare our intention and desire to become *True Women* of God. We consecrate ourselves to fulfilling His callings and purposes for our lives. Through His grace and with humble dependence on His power, we will do the following:

- We will seek to love God, our Lord, with all our hearts, with all our souls, with all our minds, and with all our strength (Deuteronomy 6:4–5; Mark 12:29–30).

- We will joyfully relinquish control of our lives to Christ our Lord. We will say "Yes, Lord," to the Word and will of God (Psalm 25:4–5; Romans 6:11–13, 16–18; Ephesians 5:15–17).

- We will be women of the Word; we will seek to grow in the knowledge of the Scriptures and live according to the holy doctrine in all areas of our lives (Acts 17:11; 1 Peter 1:15; 2 Peter 3:17–18; Titus 2:1, 3–5, 7).

- We will cultivate our communion and intimacy with God through prayer—in praise, thanksgiving, confession, intercession, and supplication (Psalm 5:2; Philippians 4:6; 1 Timothy 2:1–2).

- We will accept and express our unique designs and callings as women with humility, gratitude, faith, and joy (Proverbs 31:10–31; Colossians 3:18; Ephesians 5:22–24, 33).

- We will seek to glorify God by cultivating virtues like purity, modesty, submission, gentleness, and love (Romans 12:9–21; 1 Peter 3:1–6; 1 Timothy 2:9–14).

- We will show due respect to men and women, who are created in the image of God, considering others to be better than ourselves, trying to build them up, and putting aside any bitterness, hate, and negative speech (Ephesians 4:29–32; Philippians 2:1–4; James 3:7–10; 4:11).

- We will be faithfully involved in our local churches, submitting ourselves to our spiritual leaders, growing within the community of faith, using the gifts God has given us to serve others, edifying the body of Christ, and following His redemptive purpose for the world (Romans 12:6–8; 14:19; Ephesians 4:15, 29; Hebrews 13:17).

- We will seek to make homes that show the love, grace, beauty, and order of God, provide a favorable climate for life, and provide Christian hospitality to those outside the walls of our homes (Proverbs 31:10–31; 1 Timothy 5:10; 1 John 3:17–18).

- We will honor the holiness, purity, and permanence of marital oaths, whether ours or those of others (Matthew 5:27–28; Mark 10:5–9; 1 Corinthians 6:15–20; Hebrews 13:4).

- We will receive the gift of children as a blessing from God, seeking to train them to love and follow Jesus Christ and consecrate their lives to His gospel and kingdom (Psalm 127:3; Proverbs 4:1–23; 22:6).

- We will provide examples of piety and train those younger than ourselves to please God in all aspects, and as younger women, receive instruction with gentleness and humility, aspiring to become mature women of God who in turn will train the next generation (Titus 2:3–5).

- We will seek opportunities to share the gospel of Christ with nonbelievers (Matthew 28:19–20; Colossians 4:3–6).

- We will reflect the heart of God to the poor, the sick, the oppressed, the widowed, the orphaned, and those in prison, providing for their physical and spiritual needs in the name of Christ (Matthew 25:36; Luke 10:25–37; James 1:27; 1 Timothy 6:17–19).

- We will pray for a movement of revival and reform among the people of God that promotes the gospel and extends the kingdom of Christ to all nations (2 Chronicles 7:14; Psalm 51:1–10; 85:6; 2 Peter 3:9).

APPENDIX C

Learn to Discern

NANCY DEMOSS WOLGEMUTH[1]

The Enemy of truth is subtle and cunning. We should not be surprised by the increase in lies and spiritual errors as we near the return of Christ. The Bible says this will happen (Matthew 24:11), and God wants us to be aware of false teachings and teachers so we can stand firm in His Word. We must be discerning and not simply accept what people say is true.

BE DISCERNING: LEARN TO DISCERN BETWEEN TRUTH AND ERROR

Wisdom is the application of Scripture's truth in our lives, and God wants us to ask for wisdom (James 1:5). But discernment takes that one step further. Discernment is the ability to judge or distinguish between things using the wisdom of God's Word. This kind of judging is not wrong. In fact, it's crucial for making wise choices.

We learn to distinguish between right and wrong, good and evil, sound and unsound, and truth and error through the work of the Holy Spirit in us. The Spirit of God uses the Word of God to reveal and teach truth (John 14:26; 16:12–15; 1 Corinthians 2:13–14).

1. Adapted from Nancy DeMoss Wolgemuth, "Learn to Discern: How to Recognize and Respond to Error in the Culture," Revive Our Hearts, accessed February 3, 2025, https://www.reviveourhearts.com/articles/learn-discern-recognize-respond-error-culture/.

God praises discernment in His children. In the Old Testament, the sons of Issachar understood the times and knew what Israel should do—they were discerning (1 Chronicles 12:32). In the New Testament, Jesus told the Pharisees that they should have understood the signs of the times, but because they were more concerned with adding to the law, they couldn't discern God's truth (Matthew 16:1–3).

Adding to God's Word is always a sign of false teaching. Proverbs 30:6 and Revelation 22:18–19 clearly warn that we must neither add to nor take away from God's Word, or we will be found to be "a liar." Mishandling Scripture leads to deception and destructive teaching.

It's every Christian's responsibility to be discerning, but our attitudes in confronting error matter. We must not be hateful, argumentative, or angry. Instead, we should expose false teachings with love, kindness, and the hope of change (Ephesians 4:15; 2 Timothy 2:24–26). We must listen carefully (Proverbs 18:13) and then respond with the faithful Word (Titus 1:9), not our own opinions. God hates evil, but He also despises pride and arrogance, so our attitudes in discernment matter to Him (Proverbs 8:13).

Be Alert: Notice the Corrupting Pull of the Culture

The Bible tells us to walk carefully, "not as fools but as wise . . . because the days are evil," and to "understand what the will of the Lord is" (Ephesians 5:15–17). In other words, we need to be alert. We must recognize the errors we encounter in books, news, and media. We need to grow in our knowledge of God so we can have His "spiritual wisdom and understanding" (Colossians 1:9–10).

God's people need knowledge of His will, Word, and ways to avoid destruction (Hosea 4:6). It's dangerous to mix human opinions and philosophies with God's wisdom, just as it's foolish to substitute man-made rules for true biblical holiness. Second Timothy 3:1–5 (NIV) describes people in the last days as having "a form of godliness" while denying God's power. People are hungry for spirituality today, but they reject the holy standards of Scripture.

False prophets bring "destructive heresies," deny the Lord, blaspheme the truth, and exploit people with deception (2 Peter 2:1–3). Like the secular world, they push unbiblical values and pursue ungodly goals.

One word that confuses people today is *tolerance*. We must remember that tolerance is about how we treat people, but rationality is how we handle ideas. And for Christians, that means biblical rationality. We are not called to tolerate false ideas. Instead, we must distinguish truth from error and then expose error.

Two worldviews are in conflict—one biblical, one antibiblical. Christians are often called narrow-minded, but distinctions require a narrowing of thought. Jesus spoke of a narrow gate (Matthew 7:13–14), and Scripture makes it clear that there is no gray area when it comes to salvation and obedience.

We must expose and cast down anything that rises against the knowledge of God (2 Corinthians 10:5). Jesus is Lord of our minds, and He exercises His authority through the Word, so we must be sure we are thinking biblically.

Be Biblical: Know and Teach the Truth, and Show It in Your Life

Bank employees don't study counterfeit money; they study the real thing so they can recognize fakes. In the same way, if we want to recognize wolves in sheeps' clothing, we need to know what true sheep look like. Since evil disguises itself as truth—and Satan disguises himself as an angel of light (2 Corinthians 11:14)—we must study God's Word to recognize error quickly.

Even in some evangelical churches, people are not being taught the whole counsel of God. It's important to anchor our lives in God's character and His unchanging truth so we won't be led astray by the shifting philosophies of the world (2 Peter 1:3; 2 Timothy 2:15).

God doesn't want us to be spiritual babies. He wants us to mature in Christ so we won't be "tossed and blown about" by foolish and deceptive teachings (Ephesians 4:13–15). He wants us to grow in understanding and discernment because He hates "every false way" (Psalm 119:104).

Be Courageous: Identify and Expose the Works of Darkness

God wants us to defend the gospel (1 Corinthians 15:1) by exposing lies. We must identify the sources of error influencing us and those we love—whether it's cults, New Age thinking, or theological errors. First John 4:1 instructs us to test the spirits to determine whether they are from God. No matter who is speaking—preachers, teachers, authors, or media personalities—all teachings must be judged by God's Word (John 17:17).

The Bible describes false teachers:

- They preach another gospel and a different Jesus (Galatians 1:6–9).

- They speak from their own hearts, not from God (Jeremiah 23:16).
- They justify sin, calling evil good and good evil (Isaiah 5:20).
- They lead people astray with empty promises (2 Peter 2:18–21).

False prophets will multiply in the end times, deceiving many (Matthew 24:24). We are warned to have no fellowship with them but instead expose their works (Ephesians 5:11).

Be Prayerful: Intercede for Those Caught in Satan's Snare

Prayer is often the forgotten element in fighting false teaching. Beyond sharing the truth, we must pray that God will grant repentance to those who are deceived (2 Timothy 2:24–26). We should also pray for believers to stand firm in truth (Ephesians 6:18).

Be Proactive: Protect Yourself Against the Poison of Error

There's no such thing as a safe dose of poison. We must be careful about what we allow into our lives, and surround ourselves with God's truth. After praying for protection, we must stand firm with the belt of truth (Ephesians 6:14) and put on the whole armor of God (Ephesians 6:13–17).

With the rise of spiritual deception, we must courageously confront false teaching with confidence, compassion, and wisdom. We must know, share, and live the truth, praying that God will use us to lead others out of deception.

APPENDIX D

How to Study the Bible

The inductive Bible study method consists of answering three questions:

- What does the biblical text say? (Observation)
- What does the biblical text mean? (Interpretation)
- What must I do? (Application)

OBSERVATION

Make a Summary

After reading a passage, try to think of a title. Look for a key verse that captures the sense of the passage. Write a brief, general summary of what you have read, covering the most relevant points.

Write a Paraphrase

Try to rewrite the passage using your own words.

Ask Questions

- *Who* wrote it? Who was speaking? Who were they speaking about? Who were they speaking to?
- *What* happened? What were the main events? What were the main ideas and themes?
- *When* was it written? Have the events already happened? Are they about to happen?

- *Where* did it happen?
- *Why* was it written?
- *How* did it happen? Has it already ended?

Look for Patterns

Patterns such as repeated words or phrases can help you understand what the author wanted to emphasize.

Look Up Cross-References

As you familiarize yourself with the Bible, you'll find that when you read a passage, the Holy Spirit will bring to mind other related verses that will confirm or provide more insight about what you are currently reading.

Use Other Tools

To help you discover what the passage is saying and what it's trying to communicate, use the following tools.

- A dictionary can help you understand the basic meaning of the words.
- Other versions of the Bible can shed more light on the passage.
- A concordance can help with the meanings of words in their original language.
- Study Bibles and biblical commentaries are useful for understanding the context of the authors, the places, the characters, and the customs of the era.

Interpretation

Ask the following questions so you can better understand the implications of the text:

- What does this passage teach me about God?
- What does this passage teach me about Jesus?
- What does this passage teach me about humanity?
- Are there promises to believe?
- Are there commandments to keep?
- Are there examples to follow?
- Are there sins I must avoid?

Application

After learning the what, we must ask ourselves, "Now what?" The following questions will be of help to you:

- How can this truth be applied to my life? To my situation?
- In view of this truth, what changes do I need to make in my life?

  - Place my faith in the promises and character of God.
  - Humble myself and recognize my need.
  - Confess my sins.
  - Abandon my old way of thinking.
  - Obey those commandments that I have been neglecting.
  - Praise and worship God, who has revealed Himself in my life.
  - Forgive those who have done me harm.
  - Ask forgiveness from those I have offended.
  - Seek reconciliation in a broken relationship.
  - Be ready to give to meet the needs of others.
  - Proclaim the good news of Jesus Christ to those who are not Christians.
  - Cry out to God for my brothers and sisters in need.

NOTES

CHAPTER ONE: What Is Truth?

1. D. A. Carson, *The Gospel According to John*, The Pillar New Testament Commentary (Eerdmans, 1991), 595.

2. John MacArthur, *The Truth War: Fighting for Certainty in an Age of Deception* (Thomas Nelson, 2008), 2.

CHAPTER TWO: How Will the Truth Change Me?

1. Tim Keller, sermon, 2007 National Conference of The Gospel Coalition, cited in the article by Steven Morales, "The Bible Is Not a Disconnected Series of Stories," The Gospel Coalition, May 29, 2015, https://www.coalicionporelevangelio.org/articulo/la-biblia-no-es-una-serie-de-historia-desconectadas/.

CHAPTER FOUR: God Has Provided Everything I Need to Stand Firm

1. John Piper, "The Ministry of Hudson Taylor as Life in Christ," Desiring God 2014 Conference for Pastors, February 5, 2014, https://www.desiringgod.org/messages/the-ministry-of-hudson-taylor-as-life-in-christ#fn29.

2. See Galatians 2:20.

CHAPTER FIVE: God Is My Designer

1. Nancy DeMoss Wolgemuth, host, *Revive Our Hearts*, podcast, "Homosexuality Was Not the Only Problem," The Beauty of a Transformed Life with Jackie Hill Perry, April 3, 2018, https://www.reviveourhearts.com/podcast/revive-our-hearts/homosexuality-was-not-only-problem/.

2. You can listen to this poem on YouTube: Jackie Hill Perry, "What Is a Woman?," April 9, 2018, https://www.youtube.com/watch?v=dqXj52Xh0K0.

CHAPTER TEN: God Has Designed Me to Be Sexually Pure

1. Tim Challies, "God's Truth on Your Secret Sexual Sin," Revive Our Hearts, accessed September 5, 2019, https://www.reviveourhearts.com/articles/gods-truth-your-secret-sexual-sin/.

2. John Piper, "Battling the Unbelief of Lust," Desiring God, November 13, 1988, https://www.desiringgod.org/messages/battling-the-unbelief-of-lust.

3. *Strong's*, H3045, Bible Hub, https://biblehub.com/hebrew/3045.htm.

CONCLUSION: A Challenge for You

1. 2 Timothy 2:1.

2. Tony Merida, "Life Is War," sermon, Imago Dei Church, March 14, 2013, https://vimeo.com/61813439.